ODD FRIENDS AND ALIENS

by Franklin Zebb

Published by Temblem Publishing

ISBN-13:978-0-9575995-3-6

DEDICATION

This book is dedicated to Alena

CONTENTS

ACKNOWLEDGMENTS

Writing is an evolutionary process and sometimes you don't know what it's going to evolve into until it has already mutated! Thank you to all those people who put up with my suggestions for what happens next and to whom.

I wrote this book in the exceptionally cold conditions of the British winter and spring 2013, so I'd like to thank all my friends for keeping me well-fueled with hot drinks and heart-warming conversation.

Franklin Zebb

RAVI RETURNS

Ravi turned off the bustling high street in Stratford, East London, pulling his suitcase along by the strap. He started down the terraced street, mouthing the words to the track playing on his iPod. He felt good. Looking around, he saw a group of kids, some of them on bikes, hanging out, texting and bragging; their urban voices echoing down the street in bullet speed exchanges—the girls occasionally shrieking out in appreciation of a notable comment, accompanying this with dramatic clasps of hands across their mouths. A couple of women in their thirties, complete with designer infants in stylish buggies, walked past him, talking about some exhibition or other and a sleek, grey-haired guy jogged up the opposite pavement, glancing at his heart-rate monitor. This was East London in the twenty first Century: the Olympic Park, cool Britannia, austerity and plenty.

Ravi fitted right in to the sprawling metropolis. University was over and, although he had not landed the big job yet, he had his part-time job in Celltech Mobiles and it would only be a matter of time. Anyway, you have to wait for the right thing to find *you*: that's what he really believed —'if you've got the skill, just chill' as he liked to say. Ravi was just waiting for that call from the recruitment agency to come though, he had a degree in IT with business *and* he was on LinkedIn; before long the call would come.

He opened the front door, acknowledging the older woman who emerged from next door.

"Hello, auntie-gee," he said with a flourish. He couldn't actually speak any 'community' language very well, so, most of the time, he tended to keep his head down and pretend he hadn't seen Mrs Khan, but, with the good mood he was in, he was feeling quite tolerant with his neighbour today.

"Hah!" she responded suspiciously. "I see you're back from the visit to your family. Your friends have been playing those loud computer games again.

Mrs Khan scrunched up her face to indicate her displeasure at the thought, "These walls... " she gestured to the solid brick Victorian building next to her, "These walls are like paper."

His neighbour took another breath and was about to relay more information about the shoddy fabrication. Mrs Khan tended to feel the need to talk about the neighbourhood and the way that it was changing for the worse, quite often; Ravi knew that a blow by blow condemnation of the way that the council was wasting the excessive council tax was next, including her view that council officials were diverting some of it into their Swiss bank accounts. He tripped over the front step in his eagerness to avoid continuing the conversation, realising regretfully that it had been a mistake to speak to the older generation on this occasion. He hurried along the shabby hallway and up the winding staircase to the first floor flat. He tried the door, which gave a little but didn't open. Still, it *had* opened a couple of inches, so it couldn't have been a problem with the lock. Ravi pushed harder. Gradually the door moved open against the pile of junk that seemed to have been piled up against the other side.

"What the..." Ravi looked down the hall at the chaotic scene unfolding: a bike was lying haphazardly across the narrow corridor, magazines and paper of all sorts littered the approach to the door and clothes randomly appeared in his path. Entering the living area it got even worse. Ravi scanned the room, noting the random collections of sofa cushions flung across the floor, the empty cans, the piles of plates and the glasses. Cupboard doors were flung open and papers were strewn around the floor. The TV was still there, so maybe not all was lost; Ravi looked round frantically for his Playstation .

"Oh my God," Ravi said out loud. "We've been well turned over!" His illusion of urban perfection had been shattered.

Ravi realised that he was not as 'down with things' as he had thought a few minutes earlier. "I bet it was Romanians," he thought, "Either them or those kids down the road." Didn't he see the police at their houses all the time? Little bastards; they'd probably taken his Playstation.

"Hey Rav...Is that you? Welcome back bro'!" a voice called out from another room. "I've missed you man..."

Why was Matt so calm? Ravi couldn't detect any stress in his voice and yet the place had been ransacked – badly by the looks of it. Still, maybe he was just putting a brave face on things: Matt was always chilled out about life, after all.

"Hi Matt. Missed you too, man! What's happened, dude?"

"What d'you mean?"

"The flat...what's been taken?"

A man of about twenty slouched into the room, holding a sandwich and a mug in one hand. He was badly in need of a shave and was wearing a dressing gown over his other clothes. Despite this, he did have a sort of geeky coolness, added to by his laid back approach to what was, obviously, a traumatic break-in. Matt put his stuff down on top of a magazine and approached Ravi with a high five.

"The *flat*," Ravi said, starting to get irritated, "What have the cops said?"

"What are you on about? We just need to do a bit of a tidy up, man. It's not that bad..." Matt's voice weakened as he spoke and looked around him. He seemed to be seeing his surroundings for the first time, it was as if he had been wearing photo-chromic sunglasses that had only just adjusted to the light levels in the flat. "I guess I have let it go at bit."

"A bit!" Ravi was incredulous. "I go away for a few weeks and the place looks like a bomb-site when I get back!"

Despite Ravi's outward annoyance however, his overwhelming feeling was of relief. Thinking back, it had not been that different a couple of weeks ago. It is amazing what two weeks living at your mums does to your idea of a living environment. Ravi felt a bit guilty.

"Hey, dude. No problem!...Just checking!" Ravi did a little shuffle and pretend-boxed Matt in the guts. "Gotta keep you on your toes, you slob. Where's Doob?"

Doob was the third member of the flat. Doob was a *real* dude; a six foot, black, aspiring music producer with a cool afro. Doob was one of those guys who was sparing with conversation but witty too, if you get my drift; he mainly 'hung-out' being extremely cool and good-looking. In common with Ravi and Matt, Doob was waiting for fortune to shine and whilst he was waiting he listened to a lot of music. Doob had a DJ slot in a local club and spent approximately ten hours a day getting his set ready in his bedroom. Sometimes, young women he had met in the course of his work helped him get his set together. Everyone seemed to like Doob and, though Ravi and Matt could have been a little envious, they didn't bother—apart from being *the* best guy, Doob introduced them to the fascinating world of the London music scene, with all its dark eccentricity and excitement; without Doob they had no doubt that their world would be a lot more conventional and boring.

Ravi and Matt were *not* successful on the girl front. Most of their interaction with young women tended to be rather awkward (especially in the case of Matt, who was unemployed and didn't really meet anyone since he spent all of his time in the flat). Ravi and Matt spent much of their time playing video games, surfing the net for gadgets that they couldn't afford, or on social media sites. They had noticed that this was not something that was likely to lead to either of them picking up a girlfriend. It was not so much that they didn't *like* girls, more a kind of lack of engagement of their brains with their mouths when talking to them.

"Doob...yeah, well, he's not around bro...He's moved out"

Matt waited to see if there was a reaction from Ravi. He was waiting for a good time to break the news, but now he guessed was as good a time as any.

"Doob's gone Ravi. I just don't know where. You remember he went AWOL the week before you went away and we thought he was with a girl? Well, he ain't been back since then. Some guy came round with a letter that he said was from Doob, saying he was moving out. Someone did phone, a couple of months ago and said that he had some record thing in America and the letter said that Doob was moving to the States, so it seemed to check out a bit." Matt's explanation sounded confused.

Matt was feeling very uncomfortable. He knew that he should have called Ravi. There *were* some people that didn't like Doob. Bad people. People with guns. Doob had been threatened by a gang because of some music thing quite recently – only about six months ago. They'd stopped him on the street and said that he would be 'pinned' if he crossed some guy that Ravi had never heard of. They had even said that one day he would just 'disappear' and no one would be able to do anything about it. Doob had been careful ever since, Ravi and Matt even thought he had bought a 'piece' that he kept in his room, just in case.

"The guy said he'd squared the rent with the landlord and Doob's room was back on the market after this week." Matt continued, "He said Doob was with a girl...funny thing is, no-one seems to know who she is. And no-one we know has seen Doob since before you went away."

Ravi stood in dumbfounded silence. Ravi, Doob and Matt were

the three musketeers; they had been friends for three years, ever since Ravi and Matt had moved to London. Doob would never have left without telling them, given the circumstances.

"What the fuck Matt! Why didn't you tell me?"

Matt looked at the ground. He said nothing for a little while.

"I was going to say, but I just didn't get round to it dude. The guy even came and took some of Doobs' stuff...he said that we could keep the rest."

Ravi charged into Doobs room. The mixing decks were gone, his computer was gone and so were his clothes. Ravi looked up at the wardrobe. On the top shelf were a number of boxes, like shoe boxes, only a bit bigger. Ravi reached up and pulled one down. He opened it carefully, nervously—like a snake might dart out at him. Inside was a red leather hat.

"Doob would have wanted his hats above everything else" Ravi said, quietly, staring down at the hat with incredulity, "Something's not right."

Ravi and Matt both looked at the picture that still sat on the bedside table next to Doob's bed. It was a picture of the three of them: Ravi, Matt and Doob, arms round each other's shoulders, looking into the camera. Doob smiled out at him with his trademark charisma. Matt sat down heavily on the bed, looking guilty and troubled.

"That man, the one that picked up Doobs things, he was a bit weird," he said, quietly, "He was kinda foreign sounding. Could have been Eastern European, I guess...I'm not sure. He was wearing a sort of scarf thing too, guess that was a bit weird too— for summer."

Ravi looked at Matt despairingly.

"Don't worry, bro, we'll start looking into things from tomorrow...put the word on the street, go to the club...that sort of thing." He tried to sound encouraging but inside he felt a sense of intense foreboding—not exactly dread, more a feeling that he was not going to like what he found out. Then again, Doob *was* an adult after all; if he wanted to disappear, that was up to him. Maybe he had his reasons?

Matt looked at the photo of the three of them again. The last time he had seen Doob was when he sauntered out of the flat, saying he was going to meet 'Celia'. There was nothing after that: not even a phone call.

"There's a girl coming to look at the room tomorrow. Y'know to rent it."

"A *girl?*" Ravi didn't feel that he could cope with any more surprises.

"Yeah, you know...a girl. Not sure what her name is, the letting agent's sending her. She'll be here at ten."

"Right, Matt. We'd better start cleaning up then. Life's gotta carry on, friend."

Ravi spent much of the night trying to get his head a bit straighter. Sure, it had been a hell of a homecoming! He'd been jumped by the idea that the flat had been robbed and then the big one: what had happened to Doob?

He went over and over it in his mind. Would Doob have left completely—dropped off the face of the earth, without telling anyone? Why send someone else to get his things? Ravi ended up with more questions than answers, but he concluded that Doob might just have decided to do something wild out of the blue; there was that time that he went to that underground party for four days and no-one knew. He was probably worrying unnecessarily.

ABOUT RAVI

Ravi Patel was twenty two years old. He fitted into the category that might be described as 'British-Asian'. On forms, he resented having to declare himself to have a separate 'ethnic' identity from his friends, even though he had been born and brought up in England. Indeed, his mother and father had also been brought up in England and had lived in London for forty-five years.

In essence though, he was just a London boy and proud of it. Things had moved on considerably since the 'noughties', which seemed to him to be dominated by a general distrust of 'Asians': Ravi remembered the suspicion he faced every day getting onto the tube with a backpack. Sometimes, he'd felt that was it probably only the fact that he spent many of the journeys in the company of his friend, Oscar, that reassured fellow passengers that he was an ordinary London schoolboy making his way through the heaving, grinding city like everyone else and not a member of a terrorist group. Hearing their mono-syllabic talk on such topics as 'Sim-City'; whether to go to the fish and chip shop for lunch; or how to get out of talking in a group presentation, seemed to lower the threat level somewhat.

Actually Ravi had lived what you could describe as a rather boring life.

There was one incredible deviation from the mundane trajectory of growing up that Ravi, the teenager, undertook. When he was fourteen and a half, Ravi, his mother and father, and his brother Anil went to India for three months to visit his relatives in Delhi. His extended family was large in number, and much of the time was spent travelling across town in taxis or in his uncle's old Mercedes; arriving at one modest villa or another in a seemingly never ending schedule of visits. Ravi's extended family was indicative of the much talked about booming 'middle-class' of India: not mega-rich but aspirational.

His uncles were generally typical business-men: big, confident, well respected in their communities and well-versed in the sort of local politics that one needs to master to get along in Indian society. His aunties were generous hearted and flamboyant, showering him with concern that he was 'looking a bit thin' or needed to 'study harder' or that he should start thinking about getting himself a good wife. They usually followed the last comment with meaningful glances to his parents and references to their earlier suggestions: 'Why didn't you reply to my email about Anuka? Before you know it, Ravi will be in his thirties and all the best girls will be spoken for!'...that sort of thing.

Auntie Manjula was fair-skinned and had the ample proportions of a woman who enjoyed the extremely indulgent Indian sweets called *mitaae* a little *too* much and had taken to plastic surgery to correct things. Auntie Geeta was also fair but stick thin, her shoulders acting as a coat hanger for her stylish, close fitting, Indian dresses. Both aunties called Ravi 'beyta' and fussed over him equally, imploring him to look for jobs for their offspring in the City of London: in banking or property, for example.

Some of his cousins (both male and female) worked in software development, one was training to be a doctor and one wanted to be a commercial lawyer. Being somewhat older than Ravi, they had neither the time or the inclination to spend their free time with him and, to be honest, he was not really that bothered about cruising the fashionable streets and malls of Delhi after a while: shopping and hanging out in bars and clubs talking about ambition and celebrity quickly got a bit dull.

It was a good family, full of the vibrancy and snobbishness of the new Delhi middle class. With his easy-going, unaffected ways Ravi ingratiated himself to all of them. However, if confined to the generous but stifling hospitality of the Delhi 'set', Ravi would have quickly requested a return ticket home to London, or spent everyday watching videos in his room in self-imposed solitary confinement.

Fortunately, relief from the noise and relentlessness of Delhi was to be found elsewhere in the family tree: the family of his uncle Tanvir in Chamba, located in the northern state of Himachal Pradesh. This ancient hill town, to which a railway station was added in the nineteenth century to provide respite from the oppressive heat of the city for the colonial set, was a tourist Mecca, complete with temples and even the Akhand Chandi Palace which had been built in the eighteenth century by Raja Umed Singh. It was the classic hill-station town, with a lush green backdrop complete with deep gorges, mysterious woods, bubbling rivers and jewel-like lakes. Even the normally under-whelmed fourteen year old Ravi was left breathless with wonder as the old diesal train chugged though the landscape up to the station. The best thing about Chamba however was not the landscape: it was his cousins Ameet and Jashri.

Ameet and Jashri were brother and sister and were the children of his uncle Tanvir. Ameet was fifteen and Jashri was thirteen, so, as they were closer to his age than his other cousins, Ravi was immediately more hopeful about his stay with them. Ameet and Jashri could also speak perfect English, which helped a great deal; they spoke with a beautifully melodic Indian accent that Ravi loved to listen to. His initial fears that they would be either very childish or rather spoilt were quickly proved unfounded: Ameet was a thoughtful and adventurous friend, and Jashri was funny and highly intelligent; the sort of sister that Ravi would have loved to have had back home in England.

The summer was spent scouting the hills and foothills of Chamba, watching buffalo and wading though the rivers to get better vantage points for watching the trains as they chugged up towards the hill station and back down again. Young Ravi, kitted out in his Kurta, started dreaming about moving to India when he was grown up: to the very hill town that he liked so much. Why, he and his cousins could start a business together and they would all live happily ever after! Then something happened to shatter his summer euphoria. Something disturbing that changed Ravi's outlook completely.

Across India, small children tout wares on streets and in other public spaces to supplement the income of their families or sometimes to subsist without the benefit of a family at all. Ravi had become accustomed to their imploring faces and the raising of thin hands to their mouths repeatedly to indicate hunger—as an signal to give an extra rupee or so. Ravi usually resisted buying anything at all, since he had been warned that, should people realise that he was British, he would be hassled all the time; where there had been one meagre hand outstretched, suddenly there would be a dozen or more.

One day, however, Ravi was captivated by a little girl of about five who literally bumped into him on the market square as he was hanging around. She was running furiously, her dry tangle of dusty, dark brown hair lifting up and down as she ran and a look of determination sealed across her forehead. She caught his eye with her bright but dirty turquoise clothing and was running out of the yard when she suddenly changed direction and ran right towards him, looking into the middle distance. Ravi held out his hands as a warning. Too late. She bounced against his outstretched and fell backwards into the dust.

"Woah, look where you're going, can't you?" Ravi exclaimed, before realising that she couldn't understand a word that he was saying. Ravi looked at her frightened little face and offered her a hand to help her to her feet. As she clambered up she glanced round anxiously and appeared relieved to see nothing. She was about to run off when she seemed to remember something. Around her wrist were fastened loops of trinkets made of metal and stones: rough charms fashioned from bits of sparkling rock, worn smooth by the river. She held one out to Ravi, a linked bracelet with multi-coloured beads and a deep blue ornament of the Hindu goddess Maya on the clasp. She pushed it towards him hopefully and seemed to lose her fear, displaying her gappy, brilliant white teeth in a broad grin.

Ravi stared at the bracelet. It did look pretty, and now it came with a little story too. He imagined giving it to Jashri and telling her about the encounter in the market; it would be worth a few rupees as a talking point. What the hell, thought Ravi and reached into his pocket. He pulled out a couple of five rupee coins and handed one over. The little girl handed over the bracelet gleefully and looked at the other coin, without making any movement.

"Oh...there you are, just don't tell your friends, right?" The teenage Ravi handed over the other coin and watched the little girl skip away, apparently unconcerned about whatever had spooked her earlier.

Ravi pocketed the bracelet and spotted Ameet coming towards him, with a small dog in tow that sometimes followed people in the square.

"Hey Ravi, cousin, we're taking a walk to the caves on the side of the hills. I talked to my father and he said that this is exactly what you will enjoy."

Ameet was always incredibly thorough in planning visits for Ravi, in a humbling way that Ravi realised was not shared by many people he knew back in London. "It's not too far; we'll walk out to the caves and my father will pick us up again at the end of the day."

Ravi had certainly got a lot fitter since travelling out to Chamba; as opposed to Delhi people seemed to walk anywhere within a reasonable distance. You could understand why when you looked around you at the stunning landscape.

They spent the day talking and exploring the rocky caves dotting the hillside, venturing inside and shouting to create echoes. Ravi frequently fished out his mobile phone and took pictures of the local natural features: an interestingly shaped boulder or an unknown forest animal, for example. They threw the phone between them and snapped each other posing on the rocky outcrops, or emerging from the dark, gaping mouths of caves as they made their way around their chosen hill.

One side of the hill dropped down into a deep gorge and Ameet cautiously threaded his way around the narrow hillside path, gesturing Ravi to follow him. Ravi nervously clung on to the side of the hill. The gorge plunged down hundreds of feet below them, leaving his wrists tingling with vertigo.

"Hold on a minute, Ameet," Ravi called anxiously. "I don't know if I really want to go on." He had decided it was better to be a little humiliated by being marked a bit of a coward, than carry on feeling dizzy. He started to get the feeling that his feet were not going to move any further.

"OK, I'm coming back," Ameet's voice seemed to come from quite a way off now. "Just turn around and I will return to your location."

Ravi very slowly shuffled his feet around, whilst still clinging to the hillside with his arms, till he could hold on no longer, whereupon he flung his body round to point in the same direction as his feet. He could hear Ameet's confident steps getting closer, until he was conscious of them right behind him.

"I'm here now, cousin." Ravi felt Ameet hand on his shoulder and felt his confidence return. He started to take small steps back to the wider path.

Just at that moment, something appeared in front of him: a flash of dirty turquoise fabric and a mop of dusty brown hair. The figure jolted to a stop. The little girl looked up at Ravi and then looked over the edge to the gorge below. Quick as a flash, she flung herself over the edge. Ravi screamed out, desperately trying to get near to the path edge, but he knew it was too late. He swung round, in tears, to Ameet, who tried in vain to calm him down.

Ameet's job was made more difficult by the fact that Ravi was talking in what he thought was a delirious way—something about a girl throwing herself over the edge of the cliff, people possibly chasing her and something about buying a trinket. It made no sense at all, since he had not seen any girl or heard of any trinket-seller matching her description in the market.

Despite Ameet's belief that his cousin was suffering from some sort of delusion brought on by his severe vertigo, he did join the search party looking for the 'body' and the local police did take a report and treated the incident as serious. When no body was found however, and no-one seemed to know of the young trinket seller, the case went cold and the police moved on to their other work. Ravi managed to convince himself that he might have been seeing things and there was no little girl. Then again, there was the bracelet...

BACK IN LONDON

By the time Ravi woke up he felt relatively calm. He would start putting the feelers out for Doob but he would just play it cool for now. Hey, he had to get on with other things too and he hadn't even been online yet. He had so much catching up to do...and then there was a BIG hole in his video game schedule.

"Yo, Matt," Ravi stumbled into the kitchen looking round approvingly. "You've sure made this place shine." Actually, he didn't recall ever seeing the kitchen looking as clean: every surface was fully visible and even the dish-drainer had been emptied. Ravi noticed that the floor was sopping wet— Matt hasn't worked out how to use the squeegee mop yet, he thought to himself. Even the pages on the calender had been turned, so that it registered the correct month for the first time in half a year.

"You never know with women...and it might be nice, you know, having female company." Matt looked a bit sheepish.

"Well, the place would certainly be a lot tidier, " Ravi interrupted. " Is she the first, you know, of a few viewings?"

"They've only told me about her, but you never know. Anyway, if she wants the room I guess they'll give it to her if her references check out OK."

"I guess so, dude. Anyway, once she's left I just wanna relax for a while...I'm not at work for days, so its catch up time online. Oh, and I want to send out a few messages about Doob." Ravi had decided to start enquiries with a cautious approach.

"I wonder if she's from London" he added.

The buzzer stopped him in his tracks. Outside, a rather tallish, rather quirky-looking young woman, with long wavy auburn hair framing a robust face with strong features, stood near the front door. She was wearing blue leggings and a short black bomber jacket and was leaning to one side slightly to steady a large, old-fashioned bicycle that she had rested precariously against the front bay. The young woman looked up at the first front window above, searchingly; she pressed the buzzer again.

"Yeah, come on up," Ravi's electronic voice crackled out, accompanied by the loud entry tone.

She pushed against the door and made her way up to the flat, her footsteps echoing with the sort of clang you get when you drop a plate on a very hard surface. She paused near the door and looked behind her, as if checking that she was really there (or possibly that no-one was following?) and took a couple of deep breaths. The young woman knocked the flat door confidently. The door (which Matt had left open to try to dry the kitchen floor) swung open a little. She walked tentatively inside.

"Hello...is there anyone around?" Her Scottish accent rang down the hall, as she searched for signs of life.

Ravi scuttled out of the kitchen and into the hall. "Hi, I'm Ravi, sorry, I..." He mumbled something about not expecting her to get to the door so quickly and held out his hand.

"Hi, I'm Eleanor; people call me Ellie." She took Ravi's hand and gave it a firm shake. She smiled at Ravi, looking intently into his dark brown eyes with her blue ones and then, realising that this might be misinterpreted, pulled her hand away slightly and looked back at the door. "I've left my bike in the hall; I hope that's OK with you?" Ravi nodded that this was absolutely fine and that he was thinking of getting a bike too—probably the Olympic effect, he laughed.

I like her, thought Ravi, instantly at ease with her polite warmth. He felt that he could detect a certain efficient industriousness about her; Scottish people were known for their work ethic and Presbytarian values—right? And there was something more: something behind those blue eyes that, to Ravi's mind, seemed to fill the hall of the small flat.

He realised that he had not even confirmed that she *was* actually there to see the room and not, for example a friend of Doob's. Since Matt did not have any female friends and he'd never seen her before, this was the only other possibility—although a remote one.

"You've come to look at the room?"

"Can't think why else I'd be here!" she responded; "Prime Lettings sent me...here's my appointment letter." She held out some headed notepaper. "I'm a student at the moment, but I do some freelance work too, so no worries about the rent not being paid."

Ellie looked past Ravi's shoulder deliberately, as if to indicate that she wanted to get on with the business of looking at the room. Ravi made no movement. She seemed so familiar he thought, perhaps he had met her before? His mind started to mull over when this might have been: perhaps at university or in the mobile phone shop? Perhaps it was just her voice he was confusing with someone off the TV?

"Shall I have a look around then?" she asked, firmly.

"Oh, yeah, yeah...of course, great, I'll show you the room and then we can look around the rest of the flat. Just this way." Ravi snapped out of his loss of concentration and directed her towards Doob's old room.

"Well, this is it..." he said as he got to the door, I hope you like it," he said nervously.

Ellie looked around Doob's old room deftly. She thought it was fine, she said and made some comments about it having lots of storage space. She wanted to know if it was fairly quiet as she was a light sleeper. Ravi responded that it was now that the previous tenant had left, as he used to play a lot of music. Ellie also asked about the direction that the window faced, as she had a telescope and did some astronomy. Ravi thought this sounded 'totally awesome'.

He was just about to show her out of the room when Matt walked in. Their route out was temporarily blocked by a five foot ten and a half of confused looking geekdom.

"Hello, I'm Matt...I live here."

Matt now truly regretted deciding to introduce himself in this way. As the three of them stood trapped in the confined space, no-one was able to move very much due to the strategic positioning of the door, Matt, the bed, Ellie and Ravi.

"Hi Matt, I'm Ellie" she said, a little self-consciously.

"Yes...well, I've lived here for three years and I've got a degree in physiology," he said awkwardly. Matt was floundering a bit.

Ellie suddenly looked at Matt with genuine curiosity.

"Really, that's fascinating; I've a passing interest in it myself. Have you any idea of pathophysiology and the like?

"Not really...I mean, I did do a module in my second year." Matt said hopefully, "But that's all."

"That's a shame, that's a shame...never mind," said Ellie, speaking her thoughts out loud, "It's a brilliant subject." Ellie smiled at Matt and glanced over at Ravi.

"Matt, we'll show Ellie round the rest of the flat and then have a chat, OK?" Ravi looked competitively at Matt and gave him a slight smirk, as if to say 'yeah bro, you've cocked up your idea to make a good first impression by trying *far* too hard. Round one to the Rav'!

With a slight ducking motion Ellie wriggled past Matt who, unfortunately, had blocked her route by leaning his arm against the opposite wall. Noticing the embarrassed and slightly harassed look on Matt's face as she clambered past, she tried to lighten the atmosphere a little.

"Hey, Matt, good to meet you. Speak to you again in a bit, yeah?"

Men, she thought, they can be such idiots sometimes.

She tackled the rest of the flat with an efficiency that made Ravi think that she had already made up her mind—giving it all a verbal thumbs up, without any fuss or asking about 'issues' like cleaning rotas, communal meals, queues for the bathroom...or any of the other things that Ravi thought she might (and, indeed, that most people would) have liked to know about. She's not someone who cares too much about aesthetics thought Ravi: she's a common sense kind of person. To say that she had made a good first impression on him was rather an understatement.

The one thing she *did* ask about, when all three sat in the kitchen having a cup of tea was the broadband connection. "I'm really into computer stuff...development hacks, stuff like that," she said intriguingly. Ravi got the impression that playing video games was not really in the same league as her interests, but when she expressed a passing interest in Black Ops3 and Modern Warfare, he *had* to challenge her to a play-off.

They talked for about an hour. Ellie told them how she was studying for a research degree in artificial intelligence and that she would be at uni for much of the time, in her computer lab. She liked to go running and out on her bike and asked about where the local park was and whether it was safe. Of course, the proximity of the Olympic stadia (which had been given over to public use post the games) was a HUGE attraction.

As the conversation went on Ellie seemed to be less interested in the local area and more and more interested in Ravi and Matt, especially Ravi. As they chatted, she wove in questions about where he used to live, his studies, interests, where he worked — mentally ticking off boxes with his answers. She then got to the big one.

"Ravi, you're family's Indian, right...So have you ever been to India?" Ellie looked at Ravi with the same intensity that she had earlier in the hall.

"India, oh sure...well only once actually, about seven years ago now, when I was fourteen," Ravi was pleased that she had asked, Matt and Doob had never been that bothered about his 'Indian adventure' and he had given up trying to talk to them about it. Since the events of seven years ago he had let his contact with his relatives over there slide, partly because he had been studying so hard but mainly because he was so embarrassed to have created such a drama about the day in Chamba Hills.

"Oh, yeah...I've always wanted to go there," replied Ellie, "What part of India did you visit?"

"Delhi mainly," Ravi became a little more cautious. He was thinking about the incident with the trinket seller and, given the disbelief that people had generally greeted his story with, he did not want to say anything about it.

Ellie could sense his discomfort. There was nothing for it: she would have to go for the direct approach, even if she gave herself away she *had* to confirm whether this was him—and Ravi did not look like the kind of guy who could lie if you asked him a direct question.

"I've always wanted to go to one of those old hill station towns. You know from the days of the Raj, sort of thing...I don't know some sort of romantic notion of mine I guess. Did you go to any of those towns on your travels, Ravi?" she looked inquisitively at Ravi.

"Yeah, one"

Ellie's heart was beating loudly in her chest. She looked down at the table nonchalantly. "Which one?"

"Chamba"

Ellie had the information she needed. This really was the right Ravi Patel.

Soon after this, Ellie noticed that time was getting on; she had to go to her lab. She'd let them know about the room as soon as she could and checked that she had the right telephone number for the landlord. Ravi gave her his mobile number 'just in case'. By the time Ellie left Matt and Ravi felt as if they had known her for years. Ellie smiled up at the flat as she waved goodbye from outside the flat. She felt genuinely relieved. She had found what she was looking for.

Matt and Ravi were mesmerized by her.

"Let' not jump the gun, bro," said Ravi, watching her turn the corner out of Holly Road. "She might have a few more places to look at."

"Doob would have liked her," Matt interjected, reminding Ravi that there was unfinished business on that front and breaking the spell.

"I'm not going to let the guy down," said Ravi, feeling guilty for forgetting his friend so easily, "He's one of our crew, isn't he?...No, I'm not gonna let you down Doobie-boy, I'm gonna find you bro."

ABOUT ELLIE

There was a lot more to Eleanor Grant than she disclosed to Ravi and Matt. Nothing unusual in that—how much do you really tell prospective flatmates anyway? But it wasn't just that Eleanor had kept back the terrible, shocking truth that she left the cap off the toothpaste, or used every one else's milk: Eleanor's secrets were a great deal more interesting.

Ellie had been brought up by her grand-parents in Edinburgh. Ellie had an otherwise 'normal' childhood, attending the local primary school and spending a lot of time playing with her wee friends and visiting sites around town and the countryside. Like most grand-parents the McLeish's doted on their little grand-daughter—even more so since she had lost both of her parents in a car accident when she was a toddler; they now had the responsibility of raising her and ensuring that she discovered her potential and went as far as she could towards fulfilling it. She was the very apple of their eye.

Ellies grandparents were not what you'd call conventional. Bruce Mcleish was an eminent astronomer and physicist who had lectured at the Royal Society on occasion and his wife Elspeth was a well known local doctor and one of the leading surgeons in Scotland. Together they seemed to have enough intellect to fill St Andrews Hall, as people in the capital would say.

Until the turn of the 21st Century her grandparents enjoyed all of the recognition that thought and careful research merits in the fine city of Edinburgh—a city with a rich heritage of pioneering, particularly in architecture, the arts, medicine and science. They were lauded on the conference circuit. Bruce even became a guest presenter on the leading astronomy program of the day. Around the turn of the millennium the couple decided to wind things down and live a quieter life, away from the limelight as it were, and pursue other interests (the reasons for which will be made clear later), but when Ellie was a child they were at the height of their intellectual influence.

Of course, the young Ellie loved the opportunity to be surrounded by such a wealth of knowledge. Her young brain soaked up the fascinating sights she saw through Grand-dad's telescope and she loved hearing about how people could be repaired by Granny so that they were well again. The three of them would go walking in the Pentland Hills, little Ellie chatting away and finding all sorts of interesting treasures, before going back into Edinburgh for a welcome serving of piping hot fish and chips. This was the wonderful world of a Scottish fairytale childhood. Then one day, when Ellie was eight years old, something happened that had a profound influence on the course of Bruce and Elspeth's future, something that convinced little Ellie of her destiny...

It was five o'clock on a cold November evening and, if you've ever been to Scotland in winter, you'll appreciate just how cold it can be, especially on a clear night—which it certainly was. Bruce and Elspeth had a notion to go out for a 'wee drive', after all, it was the weekend and the bairn could have a bit of a lie in without having to worry about getting up really early for school that next day. So, into the boot of the Land-Rover went Ellie's tweed coat and her matching gloves, and woolly hat and stout little walking boots that her grand-dad had lovingly polished for her. Elspeth threw in her big, thick scarf and Bruce added his trusty deer-stalker hat and Barber jacket, oh—and not forgetting the telescope and tripod he took everywhere with him. Then they all piled into the four-wheel drive and off they went.

"Where to now then, young Ellie? I don't know where to go without your canny instructions" Bruce looked back at the young girl sitting on the back seat, expectantly, knowing that a confident reply would be delivered back to him.

"I think we should go where we can see some shooting stars," said Ellie, after some deliberation. "Somewhere, where the sky is really, really dark."

"Well, let's see now. We could go all the way over to Galloway Forest but that's too far for a bairn like you to travel to...Why don't we start going in that direction and we can go as far as we can...to Bonnybridge say and then we can drive right back and have a nice hot drink and some biscuits, just before bedtime. Deal?"

Ellie was a little disappointed. She thought that driving all the way to Galloway sounded much more exciting. On the other hand having a mug of cocoa back at home sounded rather appealing, given the temperature. Also, she knew that after an hour or so in the outdoors her feet and hands would start to get *pretty* cold despite her gloves and boots.

"OK, grand-daddy, deal!"

"Then, off we go now; let's get the old jallopy going!" said Bruce, turning the key in the ignition. Really, for an eminent scientist, Bruce was a bit of a big kid sometimes.

"Let's get the old jallopy going!" Ellie shouted excitedly, bobbing up and down on the back seat, whilst Elspeth distributed herbal cough sweets to the merry party.

"These will help ward off a sore throat in this cold. Och, it's going to be a cold one, all right," she said in her soft, Scottish accent. "Don't you try and get out of wearing your hat when we stop, young lady," Elspeth wagged her finger at her grand-daughter in a mock scold.

They sped along for about an hour, talking and laughing. Ellie told Bruce and Elspeth about the lessons she had during the week, how a boy called Barry had pulled her hair and how her best friend, Samantha, had won a prize for a story she had written. Bruce told Ellie that he was going to go to America, to a place called 'New Mexico' (which was not in Mexico at all) to give a lecture and would she like to go with them, if he talked to her teacher to get a little time off school? (Of course, Ellie wanted to go right away and wanted Bruce to ask Miss Philips, her teacher, that very night). The night got colder and colder and the sweets got fewer and fewer in number until there were none left.

"We're here!" said Bruce, turning off the engine and pulling up the handbrake with a dramatic grinding sound. "This looks the right place."

They had turned off the main road and driven along a narrow lane to what appeared to be the middle of nowhere, which was just about perfect for looking at the night sky. Ellie looked up at the sky, whilst Elspeth pulled her hat down over her face and made sure her boots were nice and snug. The inky blackness was dotted by literally thousands of tiny points of light, which appeared to Ellie to be moving now and then, making her feel a bit dizzy. She never got tired of looking at the sky.

"Wow!" Her breath billowed around her in the frosty night but she didn't feel cold in the slightest; she was just transfixed by the site overhead. However, the cold *had* affected her in one critical way.

"Granny, I need to go to the toilet..."

"Of course you do, angel, of course you do. Here, hold granny's hand and we'll find a nice spot whilst grand-dad gets his stuff out of the van. We'll just go the other side of that wall there, considering there's no-one else about."

Elspeth held out her hand reassuringly and off they went the few paces to the other side of the wall near the road's edge. Once at the spot Elspeth waited discreetly on the other side of the wall.

Ellie started to sing loudly, as she had been taught to do if she ever had to go to the toilet in the outdoors so that people would know she was OK. It was perhaps because of this that she failed to hear the small commotion happening the other side of the wall.

"I'm ready," called out Ellie after a few minutes, bounding out from behind the wall. Then she stopped in her tracks at the site that confronted her.

The Land-Rover was illuminated in a yellowish glow. Bruce and Elspeth stood either side of the vehicle, staring at the source of the light which occupied the road in front of them: an object that can only be described as a 'flying saucer', about forty feet across and balanced exactly on top of the walls on either side of the road.

"Don't move, Ellie!" rasped Bruce through the side of his mouth. "Just stay where you are and don't make a sound."

"OK, grand-daddy," said Ellie obediently and then added, "Oh, I'm sorry I spoke. I won't say anything now, grand-dad...and I won't move!"

Elspeth looked frantically at Ellie and overruled her husband. "Don't be ridiculous Bruce, can't you see the child's terrified. Come here bairn," she gestured to Ellie to move over to be next to her and Ellie rushed to huddle under her granny's coat. She *was* glad to be next to the familiar sturdy figure of her gran, but Elspeth was wrong—she was not terrified, she was very excited and curious about what would happen next.

"Where did it come from Grand-ma?" she whispered, as quietly as she could, "Is it a space-ship?" She was confident that it was, of course, but just wanted to make absolutely sure.

"I don't know what it is, Ellie. It just sort of, swooped down from the sky like a big dark bird—quiet as you like. It only lit up when it stopped atop that wall there."

"Wow!" gasped Ellie. She was in a *real* adventure. Wait till she told Miss Philips!

"Can you two stop your talking there!" croaked Bruce, "We don't know if..."

He stopped talking. A small door opened on the side of the craft and something fitting the description of a bouncy slide was lowered from the gap. Ellie was transfixed, her blue eyes wide with amazement, glued to the top of the slide. Bruce and Elspeth were also staring at the same spot. Elspeth gave her hand a little squeeze. Then they emerged.

One by one, three small creatures slid down the slide, as you might see infants doing at the play-park. The only difference being that these sliders weren't human. Well, they were kind of human but not...if you know what I mean. Short and squat they were about three and a half feet tall, greyish in colour with prominent splayed feet and proportionally very short legs and arms, with clumpy hands and fingers. They had thick necks, on top of which rested quite substantial heads with human-features (if a little elongated width-ways); in fact, they looked for all the world like a species of very small squat wrestler. It was clear that one of the figures was female (even though they were dressed in identical blue robes over their squarish bodies) since she had a feminine look about her face, long eyelashes and even a few curves interrupting her extremely stumpy looking physique.

"OH, MY GOD..." murmured Elspeth.

"Don't worry Grandma, can't you see they're friendly? Look, they're smiling at us," said Ellie, pointing at what her grandma thought was, frankly quite a uniformly grotesque expression. "Look, she's going to say something..."

The female creature (I suppose you could describe them as aliens) opened a wide mouth and started to talk. Her voice was not unlike that of the newsreader from the TV, only more croaky, thought Ellie.

"Do not be afraid: we want only to talk to you," the creature said gesturing with her stumpy arm as she spoke, "This is our vessel and we have travelled a long way to find you."

"Find *us*," said Bruce, questioningly, "You mean human-beings?"

"No, you three: Bruce Mcleish, Elspeth Mcleish and Eleanor Grant," the creature continued, "we have been waiting to talk to you. Especially you, young Eleanor." The creature looked straight at Ellie, who was trembling with amazement and cold.

"Now, just a minute there," said Bruce, "The bairns only a wee lassie. Take me with you instead."

"We do not require you to accompany us," said one of the other creatures, "We want to let you know that we may call on you in the future and that, if we do, you will not be surprised to see us."

"Well, I guess second time round it won't be *quite* such a surprise," agreed Bruce, "But why us?"

"You do not need to concern yourself with that, Bruce. We are great admirers of your work and yours too," the creature said, turning to look towards Elspeth, "You can both help us if the need arises. You can be part of the solution."

"That's good," said Bruce, looking relieved, "Just tell us what to do."

"We will communicate, when the time comes with firefly231zxspectrum, we will send you the co-ordinates of this exact location so that you know that it is us" said the female alien, "That is all you need to know, oh and you might need this..."

With that she (to the horror of the people in front of her), promptly wrapped the fingers of her right hand around one of the fingers of the other hand and snapped it off. She threw the, now detached, digit towards Elspeth, however, because of her short stature and restricted arm movement, the finger landed on top of the bonnet of the Land-Rover.

"Good God!" exclaimed Elspeth.

"Cool," said Ellie.

"We must go now. Remember: firefly231zxspectrum: all one word, no punctuation, you might want to write it down! Goodbye now." With that, they sort of bounced back inside the open door of the space-ship and seemed to wave a goodbye as the door closed.

"Wait...we don't know who you are," Bruce shouted up at the vessel, "Who are your people?"

But it was too late: the door had closed. The glow disappeared from around the flying saucer and it started to glide away. Bruce grabbed his camera off the dashboard, switched it on, and hoped that he had remembered to put film in and charge the batteries. It flashed first time. Ellie rooted around for her notebook, in which she always kept a record of the stars they had spotted, and she got her granny to carefully write: FIREFLY231ZXSPECTRUM and underlined the additional comment: all one word, small letters. Elspeth then went to the bonnet of the car, wrapped a plastic bag around the grey finger and put it into another plastic carrier. Then they all stood and looked at each other. Eventually Bruce broke the silence.

"I think it's best that we take young Ellie home and let her get some rest," said Bruce.

"I agree, the poor lass is yawning her head off there," said Elspeth, putting a travel rug over the nodding Ellie. "We'll talk about things again in the morning."

Though they spoke together about the extraordinary events of that night in November, they didn't disclose any of it to anyone else for a very long time. The McLeish's decided to ease off their work schedule, ostensibly to spend more time relaxing but really because they wanted to research as much as they could about the creatures out of the public eye: where they came from and what they could possibly want them to do.

Elspeth set up a lab in an outhouse at the bottom of the garden of their house in Juniper Green and strengthened her contacts with a few trusted friends in nearby universities who were interested in new species (admittedly, generally insects or fish) . However, she was careful never to give anyone other than herself access to the precious finger that she kept safe in a vat of nitrogen in the lab.

Bruce read all the research papers about extra-terrestrial life he could. Fortunately for him, being a renowned academic he had access to papers that most people would never be able to see. The academic side of things proved rather fruitless, so he decided to take a different approach in the hope of discovering just what the small alien creatures were. He contacted several people 'underground' using an assumed identity but discovered that most hopeful sightings were 'misunderstandings', and the few that seemed promising still drew him no closer to his goal. He drew a blank.

In parallel with this 'secret ' research' Bruce and Elspeth blended into the world of suburban Edinburgh — spending more time in the garden, visiting the sights of Scotland and, of course, following the life of their precious grand-daughter. They encouraged Ellie to continue her interest in the aliens, but they also warned her that people would probably make fun of her about it. Ellie could defend herself against ridicule, but decided to keep things quiet anyway. She would choose the people she wanted to share things with.

As a teenager, Ellie developed her passion for all things technical. It seemed amazing that, through the computer, one could have so much power to find out information, to find solutions and create change. Ellie ended up reading Computer Science at the

University of Edinburgh, before moving to London to continue her studies. As a young woman she was bright, sociable and curious about life, just as she was when she was a child. Ellie became a well known identity on the development hacking circuit—finding fixes for open source problems and even engaging in some 'subversive' information gathering.

Oh, and one other thing; she made sure she SETUred the username 'firefly231zxspectrum' on every possible available site.

LOOKING FOR DOOB

Ravi had decided that, given the fact that waiting for responses to messages would take a while, he would jump straight in and go to some of the places that Doob used to hang out, in an attempt to try to find out the truth about where is was. NO WAY was he in the United States with a girl, he had concluded: he just had too much going on in London to justify a rush departure. And the weird guy that came to the flat for his stuff...very dodgy. As Doob kept what could be described as a nocturnal lifestyle, Ravi made a plan to go firstly to the record store/audio equipment shop Doob often frequented, then on to bars and clubs later in the day and finally to the backstreet studio, probably some time after midnight. It was going to be a long day.

Ravi had met a few of Doobs mates and a few girlfriends when they came to the flat, and he hoped to God that they remembered him, otherwise the barriers could quickly come down on any questions about him. People in the dark, creative haunts of London did not take kindly to questions. If someone wanted to disappear, well it was up to them. Ask no questions etc. etc. He put the photo of Doob, Matt and himself in his jacket pocket: an insurance policy proving that he was a genuine friend. Stopping off to get some photo-copies made of another picture of Doob, to give out as posters, he walked the short distance into Stratford to see Jammo in 'Beats n' Sounds'.

'Beats was a legacy to another era—an era dating back about forty years ago to the nineteen seventies. The small shop nestled between a greasy spoon café on one side and a pay-day loan shop on the other. The only reason it was able hang on to even this humble space, given the level of commercial rent in London, was because it had what Ravi (and probably the police) believed were 'other sources of income' to those advertised to the shoppers of the local area. Beats' shop hoarding was a flaking, painted sign with 'established 1966' barely visible beneath the, by now, also barely visible name. The shop window was a strange mix of old record sleeves and technical equipment posters promoting turntables, amps, speakers and the like. Many of the record sleeves had faded in the light to yellowy pale pastels. The shop was, nevertheless, used. DJs and music buffs from all over London visited Beats, moving silently along the racks of tunes, picking out the odd sleeve and nodding appreciatively to themselves, or passing time talking to Big Frankie: the locally famous owner of the store. Big Frankie had a background in Reggae and Dub, but he seemed to know virtually everything about most types of music that had a following with his customers. Doob respected Big Frankie and Big Frankie liked Doob.

Ravi was not that bothered about music; sure he liked to listen stuff on his iPod, but mainly he just wanted something humming along in the background. Despite his lack of real interest or knowledge about music, he had, on a couple of occasions, been to 'Beats' with Doob and he hoped that Big Frankie would remember him.

"Hi Frankie, what's happening?" he ventured, walking up to the wall to wall counter at the back of the shop, behind which sat a black guy who could have been about sixty. Big Frankie was big (he had been bigger) and he had a philosophical, Buddha-like demeanour that suited his profession as a scholar of all things beat-worthy.

"Yeah...Ravi...Good to see you," Big Frankie's voice rumbled out from deep in his chest. "I haven't seen you for a llonnnggg time, young man! What's happened to Doob, man?"

"I was hoping you could tell me..."

Ravi had anticipated that Doob would have vanished from his other haunts, as he had from his home, nevertheless, he felt a pang of disappointment that Frankie was confirming this.

"I ain't seen the guy for months, man," Frankie looked at Ravi's face, "You OK?"

"Yeah, no...Actually Frankie, Doobs gone missing. People put the word out that he's gone to America, something to do with a record job..."

"America?..No man, it ain't possible! I know the US network and there ain't no way Doob's over there without me knowing about it. Get it? No, no, the boy's got too much going on here man: with the club and all that shit. I even set him up with that record production job with Jammo in Lewisham...No man, ain't no way the kid's gone to America."

"Well, where is he then?" Ravi looked blankly at Big Frankie. He told him what had happened; when he got to the part about the strange guy that had come to the flat, ostensibly having been sent by Doob, Frankie interrupted him.

"There, you see what I mean? That there proves it, Doob's not gonna leave those hats behind. Those hats is his *Marcus Garvey* collection. Bet Doobs gotten himself into trouble...Shame, he don't seem the type to get mixed up in any nasty business." Frankie looked disappointed. Why did all the promising kids seem to go bad nowadays? He didn't understand it.

"You're right—he's not that type," said Ravi.

"Look, kid, anyone can get involved in trouble if the stakes is high enough. Get me?"Big Frankie couldn't give Ravi any more information; or he didn't want to.

Realising he had gone as far had he could in the conversation, Ravi took out a photo of Doob and handed it over, asking Frankie to display it behind him, in case anyone had seen Doob around.

"Don't worry, man," Big Frankie reassured Ravi, "I'll keep listening and get the feelers out. You go to Jammo's and The Red Club—and talk to Angel, she might know something. Look, Ravi, I'm not messin' with you, if I knew where the guy was at I'd tell you, right? If I hear of anything I'll let you know, OK?"

Ravi was already heading for the door. He needed to visit a few more stores before catching Angel at Beluga for lunchtime.

By the time Ravi got to Shoreditch, home of the famous Beluga Martini Bar, he had distributed the photo-copies of Doob around several other music-themed outlets, ranging from promoters to music bloggers. He also left word with DJ T-Ray of Sunrise radio, operating out of New Cross, the channel that serious musos like Doob tuned in to. T-Ray said that he would put a shout out for Doob on air and spread the word using the code language that the underground scene would understand. Despite the concern and apparent willingness to help, Ravi had drawn a blank.

Beluga was an upmarket Martini bar in a fashionable location It stood on one corner of a pedestrianised square and, looming over the adjoining wealth with its Gaudiesque design, its dark interior and the over-sized copper tables and leather seating visible from the street: enticing the uber-trendy into its velvety folds. Angel was a girl *friend* of Doobs who worked at Beluga as a hostess. She was not an ex-girlfriend: she was a friend who happened to be a girl. Angel and Doob went back a long way and there was no-one (not even his mom, he used to say) that knew Doob as well as Angel. She had agreed to meet Ravi before her shift and ushered him past the onyx fittings and mirrors to the staff rest-room, next to the expansive and labyrinthine private bar area in the basement.

Angel was a short, curvy girl with precision-waved blonde hair and a cherubic look to her face. She had a vintage look about her, which was accentuated by her bright red lipstick. Angel was, by all accounts, a backing singer in her spare time and had appeared with several well-known artists. She and Doob had a fiery friendship, full of ups and downs, but they also had a pact that they would get a music business together and make it to the big time one day; then they'd move over to California and everyone would come and stay in a big house that they would buy. Angel was always dreaming.

"Look, Rav, I haven't got much time but I'm so glad you're here," she said hugging the bewildered Ravi in the store-cupboard sized room. "It's about Doob. He spoke to me about two months ago and told me he was gonna do a job for Jammo, and to get ready for the big time and then he just...left." Angel wasn't making much sense. She thought maybe Doob *had* gone away, after all he was a free agent; he'd spent time 'underground' before, hadn't he? Then she remembered something.

"He left something at the bar for me to give to you one day; but you've not been around so..."

Ravi straightened his back and started listening intently: at last, a breakthrough.

"For me?...But why didn't you bring it over? No-one knows where Doob is, Angel: whatever he gave you could be important," Ravi looked incredulously at Angel. She looked at the floor.

"You know how it is, hun. I was annoyed with Doob for not telling me anything and just going like that; you'd have thought that he'd have included me in his plans," Angel had obviously been hurt by Doob's sudden departure, but since then her feelings had changed to those of concern: "I thought Doob would be back by now though. I kept trying to get back in touch with him, and, when he didn't reply, I kind of spent more time worrying about that than thinking about giving you whatever."

Angel stepped over to a bank of grey metal lockers against one wall and unlocked one, rummaging about through a pile of assorted junk until she found a brown paper package, neatly box-shaped and marked 'Ravi' on the top. She handed it over to him.

"Look, I'm so sorry, Rav, but Doob didn't even say anything. I didn't even see him. He just left the package with Carlo at the bar, and it took Carlo a week to give it to me..."

Ravi was not listening to her: he was tearing open the wrapping from the box. He lifted the lid and looked inside. He carefully took out the contents. In the box was a pair of headphones. After all that it looked like the package was just Doob giving him his old phones to replace the regular ones that he knew Ravi was always moaning about. It was a dead end. No clues, nothing.

"Well, there's no problem with getting these a bit late, Angel. You can breathe easy, sister," Ravi said, seeing that Angel was looking upset.

Ravi stuffed the packages into his bag and swung it across his shoulder. "Look, I'm gonna go home for a bit, cos I'm heading out later to check out Jammo's. If I hear anything I'll let you know. Stay strong girl."

Angel had sat down and had her head in her hands. She wasn't interested in the stupid package, she just missed Doob.

"Look, I'll see myself out, " Ravi had already walked out of the room and retraced his way up the opulent spiral staircase to the main lounge room. He was about to step out onto the street when he turned back and walked up to a very good looking young man, possibly of Mediterranean origin, standing behind the bar.

"Are you Carlo?"

"Si, I mean yes, Sir."

"Do you remember someone leaving this package?" said Ravi, fishing out the parcel from his bag.

"Yes, Sir, it was a few weeks ago."

"What did the person who gave you the package look like?"

Ravi waited with baited breath.

"He was a Polish guy, I think...I'm not sure," Carlo hesitated, "I did not understand too well because he was no English, but I think he say it was for Angel from her friend. I don't speak English too good, myself.

"So it was not this man?" Ravi asked, showing him the grainy photo-copy of Doob.

"No, Sir...not this man. It was another man."

This is getting worse and worse, thought Ravi. I need a drink

Back at the flat, Ravi cracked open a glass of beer. OK so what did they know: Doob had disappeared, some Eastern European guy had removed his things but left his hats, possibly the same Eastern European guy had left Doob's headphones for Ravi at Beluga, no one seemed to have heard from Doob for two months. It made no sense.

Ravi remembered that both Big Frankie and Angel had mentioned that there was a possible job lined up with Jammo. He'd follow that up that night. He needed to take his mind off things for a while: perhaps a bit of gaming...?

That evening Ravi headed out to some of the after-dark venues that he knew that Doob was a regular at. Admittedly, it was not the way that Ravi liked to spend his leisure time, but it had to be done. He had to get some clues about what had happened to Doob. He got a tube down to New Cross and started asking at some of the back street hang-outs, ignoring the folded arms of the bouncers and the occasional suspicion raised by an Asian lad going around asking over the whereabouts of a 'black' guy. Ravi was pleased that he had the picture of the three of them together to show around.

Most people knew Doob—he had the chat to make friends easily and the looks to make friends with girls, as Ravi acknowledged. The problem was that Doob's world was not exactly renowned for stability: people just drifted in and out again without leaving much of an imprint.

Doob was not into the sort of turf warfare and gangland that certainly existed in the city, he was only interested in the music. However, becoming caught up in things was easy enough. Perhaps Doob *had* become mixed up with the wrong crew? Eastern Europeans were now right in the thick of things in the East-End: maybe something had kicked off and Doob was caught in the proverbial (or real) crossfire? Scores were settled all the time and mistakes made. With the police overstretched it would not take much of a cover-up for them to lose interest, if they had any in the first place. Ravi shuddered, I hope I don't have to start down that line of enquiry, he thought to himself, realising that, unfortunately, this sounded like the most likely course of events that he had mooted thus far.

His enquiries at clubs had drawn a blank. No-one had seen Doob for over two months and life seemed to have moved on for people in most of his old haunts. There was the occasional hint that someone might have seen him somewhere more recently but everything was too vague. He needed something more concrete.

Ravi walked down Lewisham Road, leaving New Cross behind and went through Lewisham and into Catford, which is where Jammo had his studio. This was not a studio as most people outside the music industry would imagine it, but it was typical of the kind of rough and ready set-up that many emerging artists recorded in at the bottom of the music hierarchy, many never progressed past this level. The 'studio' was literally a sound desk in the front room of Jammo's house, with a small, tardis-shaped booth equipped with a microphone in one corner; a window cut out on one wall of the booth and filled with transparent plastic so that the singer could see the producer at the desk. The booth was lined with egg boxes to improve the sound-proofing.

Despite the rough and ready look of the place and the fact that the house obviously doubled up as a place to score weed, Jammo had launched a number of successful acts from his front room and he was (the last that Ravi had heard) very keen on taking Doob on as his sort of resident producer.

Ravi had never met Jammo, but he no doubt that even in the course of a day, word would have spread that he was asking questions about Doob. He hoped that Big Frankie was genuine and had cleared Ravi as being 'OK' before any of the rather dodgy characters that he had met in the evening had talked to Jammo and warned him off talking. Regardless, Jammo had a reputation of being an unpredictable and independent-minded man. He was likely to go with his own instinct—if he considered anything to be an issue at all.

Ravi waited in the living room alongside about six or seven guys who seemed to be hanging out in the house, smoking weed and drinking beer or fruit juice out of cartons. Some girl was in the sound booth and a young guy with short dreadlocks was at the sound desk. Apart from the instructions to the singer, no one was saying much; Ravi felt very conspicuous. Just then Jammo walked in, Ravi knew it was him from Doob's description: a tall, wiry man with long dreads and a deeply furrowed, intelligent face. He looked straight at Ravi and gestured to him to follow him. He called out in patois to the men in the studio and they answered him raucously and started to talk and gesture to each other. The ice appeared to be broken.

Ravi followed Jammo to the kitchen of the house, where Jammo casually leaned against the counter.

"Wa a gwaan, Ravi…Relax, you look scared—man!" Jammo let out a hearty laugh, displaying his gold front tooth and leaning towards Ravi, "Hey, you got nothing to be scared of, blood. I've been waiting for you." He pointed a long finger at Ravi and laughed again, shaking his right hand so that the fingers snapped together with a sharp rapping sound. "You seeking Doob, blood? So is I! but I and I already got a head start bredren!" Jammo looked at Ravi as he continued his animated delivery. Ravi stood, watching Jammo, spellbound.

"Doob sent me message last week, blood! He say he good and he's with a girl and he send me this picture of this short-ass little sista, kinda pale, y'know not really my type—too damn skinny." Jammo erupted into laughter again. "He never told no body cos, well, some t'ings people don't need to know till they find out—right?"

Ravi thought this was a bit of a lame excuse, considering that so many people appeared to be worried about where Doob was, but he didn't mention anything. It all sounded more and more strange.

"That's great Jammo, but I just wanna check things out, properly. It all sounds like things are moving from one thing to the next with no connection... Mind if I see the message?" he wanted to make sure it was Doob.

"Undastan...It right here," Jammo scrolled down his phone, "Here, man. Here it is." Jammo pulled up an image and there was Doob, looking cool as ever. It was a Youtube style video.

"Hey, Jammo, Wa a gwaan? Can't talk for long 'cos I'm busy with music. I'm cool. With my new friend—I'll send you a picture, give it to Ravi." then Doob looked a little to the side and his expression changed as he said, "I need a break from playing: tell Ravi to help me out, man."

That message could have been recorded at any time, thought Ravi. He had hoped for something a little more conclusive.

"Playing?..I didn't know that Doob played an instrument..."

"No...yute... he mean playing the decks, I and I believe."

Ravi was encouraged, but this was still far from an authentic, in the flesh, identification. He needed to think about things.

"D'you think you could send me that message and the picture of the girl?"

"No, problem!" Jammo wanted to see Doob as badly as Ravi.

They exchanged message addresses, Ravi declined the offer to stick around for a while and he made his way home, still with many unanswered questions.

It was a long, slow bus ride home, and Ravi sat on the top deck of the number 108 bus, looking out of the window as the bus wound its way through darkened London streets, first through Blackheath, then Greenwich and then Poplar. It was after two in the morning, but London never sleeps, and there were still people making their way to and from places, mostly pretty wearily. Ravi found himself looking around intently at everyone that might remotely be Doob, half expecting him to get on the bus and sit next to him. He had covered all of the immediate bases and there was nothing else he could do now. Even if the message from Doob was genuine, it gave no indication of where he was, what he was really doing, or when he would be back. In short it was pretty damn useless.

ELLIE MOVES IN

The next day came the news that Ellie was actually and really moving in to the flat. The landlord had OK'ed it for her to move in that weekend, since all of the banking details had been cleared. It turned out that one of the women that worked for the letting agency was also from the town that Ellie was raised in in Scotland, so she had taken care of ensuring that all the paperwork was expedited promptly, herself.

Matt and Ravi were pleased, both because they felt somewhat captivated by Ellie's charm and seemingly unaffected ways and, secondly, because they didn't want to show any more people around the flat. They spent a bit of time speculating about the key fact of whether she had a boyfriend: both of them agreed that it was unlikely. This was not just hopeful thinking but based on the fact that they had spent over two hours in each other's company and she had not once mentioned anyone that could be labelled in this way.

She had described her research as "something to do with linking the philosophy of intelligence to cognitive simulation." This sounded terribly important. Matt had looked up 'philosophy of intelligence'... obviously, he had only accessed general sites about philosophy and had proceeded to annoy Ravi with random philosophical statements such as:"The unexamined life is not worth living" "One cannot step twice in the same river" and his personal favourite, obviously "Leisure is the mother of philosophy." Ravi was becoming increasingly annoyed with Matt's new incarnation as an armchair philosopher.

Ravi had other distractions. He had received the message from Jammo and had been viewing it over and over again on his laptop. He had also collected Doobs hats, the headphones from the package given to him by Angel and the photos of Doob on the table in his room and kept looking over them, waiting for something to leap out at him by way of a solution.

The message was only a few seconds long and yielded no real clues as far as Ravi could see. Doob's words could have been cryptic but, then again, they could just have been vague. He said he was doing his music and with 'some girl', thought Ravi: it sounded plausible. Then again, what 'girl'? What 'music'? Even with sophisticated expert equipment there was no way he was going to be able to find out where the video was taken (it appeared to be in possibly a motel room of some sort, a bit plasticky looking—you know the sort of place). Ravi looked carefully at Doob's face whilst he was talking. He thought he detected a real change at the point after Doob had glanced to the side: after this point he seemed to look deeper into the camera—with an urgency that did not match the casual words.

"Looking forward to playing with you guys soon," repeated Ravi, ponderously. "Where ARE you Doob?" he said out loud.

Ellie moved in and for a few days kept herself to herself, setting up her room and taking numerous trips out on her bike, often returning with curious items wrapped up in plastic carrier bags. One time Matt decided that he would take a look into one of these mystery packages, since she had carelessly left it in the kitchen rather than taking it to her room. He was disappointed to find that, on this occasion, it only contained a jar of coffee and a large bag of crisps. They could hear her tapping away on her computer and talking in a hushed voice on the phone, often repeating "a-ha, a-ha" in acknowledgement of what the other person was saying.

Like Ravi, Ellie had also collected items. Her items were part of an ongoing puzzle and the reason for her arrival at the flat in East London. The information she had given Ravi and Matt was all correct, she *was* doing researching at Queen Mary College and she *did* have all of the interests that she had described, which would have made the flat in East London a perfect choice of residence in all respects. However, the main reason that she had moved in was not the proximity of the flat to the university, or to the Olympic Park, or even the vibrant diversity of the area—the reason that she had moved in was Ravi.

Ellie sat at the small desk in Doob's old room, now her room—and propped her tablet on its stand. Ellie was what you might call a gadget freak. Since the age of thirteen she had possessed her own computer. If she had wanted it she would also have had access to some of the most powerful computer systems in the world. However, this was not required. She had set up a hack so that she automatically joined new social networks. She had written to the exact user name given by the aliens and fired it off. All she had to do then was wait until someone (or something) contacted 'firefly231zxspectrum' with the co-ordinates of that road on the way to Bonnybridge.

She fired it up and started typing, using the separate keyboard that she found it easier to work with. A few seconds later, she was in the account that domino236ot' had used to get in touch with her with the exact co-ordinates of the point on the road at which they had stopped. She looked back though the messages. One by one the interchange unfolded, always initiated by 'domino236ot' and always short. The dialogue was not frequent, or regular, in fact periods of years went by between messages. The first, with the 'code' of the co-ordinates, had appeared in the year 2003, followed a few days later by:

"We are looking for the right challenge."

She (or rather firefly231zxspectrum) had sent a number of messages back, trying to find out more about what the 'challenge' might be. What sort of challenge was it? It seemed like a *very* obscure message; but then what was she expecting. There was nothing for it but to wait for more clues: that was fine, it was becoming more interesting. Then, a few years later, came a succession of messages:

"We have heard from Ravi. "

Ellie started looking for 'Ravi'. She needed more, something that might identify this 'Ravi' by something more conventional. A surname would be a start (although given the sheer number of Ravis and Ravinders and the complexity of Indian naming, even that was likely to be of limited help). A location would be better; an age; confirmation that 'Ravi' was male—all of these things would be some help. Then, shortly afterwards, a breakthrough!

"We acknowledge Coolio345londonboy, Ravi has chosen a good name" came the message.

At last, something to go on. Not only was this a possible username, it could also possibly pinpoint Ravi to a city—and a city not that far from Edinburgh!

The seventeen year old Ellie was, by now, well and truly established in a number of underground hacking networks, and she knew that if the username existed she would be able to call on support to find it. She did a basic search on her own: nothing. She used a few different techniques, but still Coolio345londonboy did not show up on any lists.

Ellie decided to open up the enquiry. There were specialist groups of hackers who made it their life's work to track down people behind user names, sometimes they even helped the police if they were looking into paedophile rings, scammers and the like. Ellie threw the username into the court. She said nothing about why she needed to find who Coolio345londonboy was—that was not needed. You did not have to reveal why you needed to unmask the user. The challenge was enough.

It only took a matter of a week and the secret was revealed. A message pinged into her inbox with the response, sent from a hacker in Germany: Coolio345londonboy was a schoolboy living in London at the time that the name was in use. He had used the username for a class assignment in a South London Education Authority in 2004. It was normally quite difficult to get information that related to school user names, but in this case her hacker contact had been lucky—to an extent. The account had only been used for a few months and after that they had been deleted (presumably at the end of the course). Unfortunately, that was all the information that could be found. Ravi's surname was not available and neither was the school's name. Still, Ellie had come a long way: Ravi had been tracked down to London!

The downside was that there were literally hundreds of potential 'Ravis' attending school in London in 2004. She was going to have quite a bit of detective work to do and, with no more clues, how would she know who he was? Did he know something himself, she started to wonder; perhaps if she contacted all the possible Ravis, one of them might respond? It could even be that he was on a similar mission looking for *her*.

There was no further contact from domino236ot for the next four years. Ellie decided to put the matter to one side whilst she studied and learnt about things that she was both interested in and might help her with what had become her major quest. She became more and more interested in ideas about intelligence and whether other species might exhibit skills that sounded fantastical: especially the ability to influence the future from the past. Could it be that the creatures that she had met were able to travel through time...to control what happened in some way? It was too mind-boggling to comprehend.

Ellie knew she was fortunate that her grand-parents did not pretend that night, over a decade earlier, had not happened. Though they kept things fairly low key externally, for fear of jeopardising their mission (the mission that they were convinced would reveal itself over time) the three of them would meet and talk from time to time about any progress they had made in finding out who the 'others' were or, indeed, who the mysterious Ravi was and why he was so important to the alien creatures.

Then, four years after the breakthrough message with Ravi's username, came the next clue. One evening, whilst Ellie was reading and listening to music in her room at university her phone bleeped. Ellie reached over automatically, without taking her eyes off her book. When she saw who the message was from however, and what it said, the book dropped out of her lap and onto the floor.

"We are pleased that Ravi chose to accept the Blue Goddess in the Chamba Hills. The child who gave it is with us"

Ellie was straight on the case. Had Ravi visited these Chamba Hills?—had something happened there? Her research led her to the Chamba Hill range in northern India. She started to call upon her anonymous friends to help her work out if any of the Ravis on her list had been to India during the last say ten years or so? The answer was yes—quite a few of them. There were still left over a hundred Ravis left in the frame. Then she had an idea.

Ellie contacted a group of student hackers in Mumbai. She asked cryptically if anyone knew of any incidents in Chamba involving a child and the possible connection to a deity or goddess of some sort. An answer came back from someone called 'Ameet'. His cousin had witnessed a child fall over the side of a cliff a few years ago. The case was now closed as no-one found anything and no-one was reported missing. Ellie asked him the question and then waited nervously for the answer. The answer came the next day. Ameet's cousin's name: Ravi. He lived in London.

That is how Ellie strung together the links that had now brought her to Holly Road . Ellie looked at the small list of messages once more. So few. They had apparently been sent from an IP address in France, but that was irrelevant: the sender must have used an IP mask. She was sure that whoever sent the messages was not some French guy feeling a bit bored.

Ellie switched off her computer and went to the window. She had set up the small telescope that her grandfather had given her but with London being just about the worst place you would want to be to see *anything* in the sky, she did not hold out much hope to do any viewing. Never mind, she thought to herself, I've got other things I need to do.

SPILLING THE BEANS

Over the next week or so, nothing notable seemed to happen. Ravi continued to think about where Doob could be. He went back to the places that he had left the pictures of his friend but no-one— Big Frankie, Angel, Jammo or anyone else, seemed to have heard anything new. Matt seemed to take everything in his stride, just easing back and reading through the job websites...just reading stuff in general. He had taken an interest in artificial intelligence to find favour with Ellie and found that the whole topic was pretty mind blowing (he had also started looking into pathophysiology and found that a little bit more difficult). Ellie appeared to be working hard and spent a lot of time in her room when she was not at university.

Ravi got the distinct impression that Ellie was looking at him sometimes; to be honest it had started to become slightly disconcerting. However, he put it down to the fact that he was on edge about Doob and possibly becoming a bit paranoid as a result. He realised that Ellie knew nothing about the disappearance of Doob (she didn't know Doob and he didn't want to freak her out about it). Perhaps I should say something about things? he thought to himself.

The whole thing preyed on his mind until, a few days later, Ravi decided to tell Ellie about the mystery involving Doob, possibly more to get it off his chest than anything else. It was one of the rare occasions that Ellie was not in her room. She'd just popped in to the kitchen to make a cup of tea.

"Fancy a brew, Ravi?" she asked, cheerfully, "I've just put the kettle on."

"Please," said Ravi, "Hey, Ellie are you settling in OK?"

"Fine, thanks."

This was terrible. Both of them had things they really needed to tell each other and yet they had only succeeded in talking in pleasantries. Ravi took a deep breath.

"Ellie. I wanted to talk to you..."

"Ye-es," Oh, my God, thought Ellie, he knows about *them*.

"It's about the person that used to have your room."

"Yeah, a guy called Doob wasn't it?"

"Yeah, that's the guy. Well he didn't just move out. What I mean is, he moved out but not in the way that most people move out, at least I don't think so"

Ravi told Ellie about the weird events surrounding the departure of his friend Doob. To his surprise, she didn't seem the least bit freaked out by any of it, though she did seem very concerned.

"And you say that no-one has actually *seen* Doob for some time, even though some people have claimed to have been contacted by him?" Ellie articulated each phrase with precision, making absolutely sure that she had the story right.

"Yeah, that's right...I've just got the the stuff I just told you about: the headphones, the hats, photos—oh and that message that Jammo passed on.

"Can I see it?" asked Ellie.

"What the message?"

"No, well yes—but everything else too. I want to see whatever you have got."

Ellie seemed to Ravi to have acquired the demeanour of some sort of senior detective: she had the aura of someone who would take one look at his 'evidence' and solve the puzzle, he thought.

Ellie looked carefully at each item that lay on Ravi's desk. She picked up the photo and peered at Doob's confident, handsome face; she looked at the ostentatious hats and the few old vinyl records that had also been left behind. Ellie had friends that were into music and she knew that there was no way that a muso would not ask for 'white labels' such as these to be packed up and passed on to them. Even if they had been forgotten, Doob would still definitely have asked his friend in the business 'Jammo' for them when he made contact.

She looked at the headphones, pretty cool, she thought. They were fairly vintage but high quality 'DTs', the sort used in studio work.

"So there wasn't any sort of note or anything...just your name on the package? Kinda odd don't you think...considering, the guy is giving you quite a hefty gift and hasn't seen you for months?"

Ravi hadn't even stopped to think about a note or a letter. He was so intent on chasing round town looking for clues about Doob that he had overlooked something quite basic. He admitted to Ellie that he had not really looked for any message.

"Where's the box they were in?" Ellie asked, looking around the room.

Ravi picked the box up from under the bed and opened it up. Inside was scrunched up tissue paper. He turned it upside down and the tissue tumbled to the floor. Along with it floated a flat piece of white paper. Ravi caught it before it reached the floor. On it was written:

"Ravs—thought you might want my cans...Doob"

Well, at least it wasn't something critical that they had missed: it was just a regular scribble.

Ellie had moved on to the video of Doob—the one that Ravi got from Jammo. She had already downloaded it onto her own phone, so that she could look at it in her own time. Anyone can see that's a set-up, she said to herself as she watched it: the whole things wrong.

"...and there's no picture of this 'girl' yet, the one that Jammo said was 'not his type'?" she asked Ravi.

"No, none."

"Can I have a look at your email account?"

Ravi logged into his notebook and opened up his account. Ellie made a few clicks here and there, and up popped a mail.

"In the junk folder," she said, turning the laptop over to Ravi, "Don't worry, it happens to me all the time. I'm always forgetting to check." The mail had no content but there was an attachment. Ravi clicked on it and squinted at the photo.

"I don't know if Jammo's got bad eyesight, but that's one hell of a weird looking girl! Do you think she's in fancy dress?"

Ellie peered over Ravi's shoulder at the short, pale, squat figure in the totally unflattering pink dress.

Is she *smiling*? thought Ellie. There was no mistaking what was captured on the picture. It was one of *them*! Ravi had named the attachment 'Shaz'. Ellie decided to stick with this name—at least then she would be able to call them something; 'Shaz' seemed to fit their look quite well.

Ravi was staring and staring at the image. She really was not normal looking—and that was the girl that Doob had left to be with? He didn't think so!

"She's not his usual type..." Ravi said, understating the difference considerably. "He usually likes...taller girls."

"Ravi, lets go into the other room and talk, I've got a few things to tell you. For a start, that 'person' is not human: I've seen others like her," Ellie paused in case she was coming across like a total fruitcake, but Ravi looked as if he thought that this was completely plausible, given the picture.

"OK," he squeaked. Things had been pretty weird and they were getting weirder by the minute.

Ellie made a cup of tea and they sat down in the living area.

"Ravi...This is all going to sound very, very strange, but hear me out. It doesn't make sense to me either, if that helps."

Ellie started to go though the events of the night fifteen years ago, when she was eight years old and went for a drive with her grandparents, for the purpose of star-gazing. She described the 'flying-saucer' and the three creatures who looked just like the female 'Shaz'. Ravi, it has to be said, was not really convinced by the story and started to look at Ellie like she had totally lost the plot. Ellie continued, regardless, swallowing hard. This was going to be harder than the 'best case scenario' that she had imagined.

"Look, Ravi, the next bit's about you. It is really important that you believe me on this," Ellie looked imploringly at Ravi. He nodded.

She told him about the contact that had been made with the 'Shaz' and the way that she had used her contacts to filter things down, until she had concluded that he must be the Ravi in question. It was when she got to the part of her story about the girl in the Chamba Hills and Ameet that Ravi changed. He had never forgotten that day and the eerie emptiness left where the little girl had been standing a few seconds earlier. On balance, thought Ravi, there does seem to be quite a lot that can't be logically explained *unless* Ellie's story is true. How could she get those messages that clearly pointed to him...and the disappearance of the little girl? More than anything, Doob's whereabouts were clearly linked to these 'creatures' and Ellie would have known nothing about that before she came.

"I've got this," said Ellie, fetching something from her room. It's a copy of a photo my grand-dad took on that night." Ravi looked at the very grainy and dark picture. It was a large object about the size of a house but saucer shaped, floating above the person taking the picture. Clearly visible was a window of some sort, facing down and in the window the pale figure of something that was very similar to the photo they already had of the 'Shaz'. Ravi looked at the picture and at Ellie. She had spent such a long time and come such a long way to find him. He felt humbled all of a sudden.

"Ok—I'm in," he said, carefully. "I don't know what I'm in—but count me in!"

Ellie breathed a sigh of relief. She had not fully figured out just how she was going to tell Ravi that she had been looking for him. The reality of it had been, she concluded, not as bad as it could have been—thanks to the unfortunate situation with Doob.

"What happens now?" asked Ravi, looking straight at Ellie.

"We wait for the Shaz to contact us Ravi, don't worry it will happen."

To be honest, Ellie had not properly thought about what was going to happen once she had found Ravi, she just knew that finding him was important. Everything that she had seen and heard since being in London confirmed it. Her hunch that they would not have to wait long for the next stage of the drama proved to be all too correct.

DISRUPTION

Ellie had volunteered her contacts with the underground world of hacking to the service of finding clues about where Doob could be, although she, personally, felt that he was probably going to prove pretty hard to track down. She got online and sent Doob's video message out to a few trusted friends, but nothing came back that would prove helpful. She did not send the picture of the 'Shaz' to anyone.

Ravi and Ellie decided that they would have to let Matt in on what was happening: it was going to be pretty hard to conceal stuff going on in the house anyway, and three heads are better than two. Matt, in his usual laid back way was absolutely un-phased and wanted to help in any way he could. Ellie told him to start looking into a number of obscure physiology texts that her grandmother, Elspeth, had recommended. Matt took this very seriously and, since he had a lot of time on his hands and *far* greater motivation that when he was at university, actually understood what he was researching really well.

Matt was one of those people who might be termed 'slow burners'—methodically ploughing through information and embedding key facts in his mind. Matt was one of the world's nice guys, given the opportunity he would definitely have worked for free for some charity or other; money was never a high priority. Sure, he played second fiddle to Ravi and probably third fiddle to Doob, but he knew his own worth and contributed as much as he could to the team effort to make something happen.

Whilst Ravi was at work, Ellie and Matt had set up a link to Bruce and Elspeth. Matt had sacrificed his treasured gaming monitor to use as a screen, so that they could see each other properly, and so that Elspeth could show them some of the experimental results that she had performed on some of the precious tissue samples she had taken from the finger.

Bruce and Elspeth had finally taken the decision, about three years ago, to open up their interest in the 'extra-terrestrials' to a few more people. Since retiring, they had drifted out of the public imagination somewhat and were 'under the radar' as it were; important in terms of keeping the wrong sort of attention away, whilst attracting the 'right' kind of interest and help. Bruce had, over the years, worked out which of the many feelers he had out, had reached people who were worth speaking to; people reluctant to speak despite the strength of their evidence. Bruce and Elspeth had both, using their Scottish charm and credentials, made use of their contacts in the academic world—via just a few people they were able to access statistics, reports and, sometimes, classified information. They were particularly interested in the message from Doob and the photo of the Shazette (as Ellie had termed her).

Do you think Ravi is OK?" Ellie asked Matt as they pored over the documents that littered the living area (the flat once again resembled the state that it had reached when Ravi had come back from his holiday, only for legitimate and important reasons this time). "He's been looking a bit stressed."

"Yeah..I think so," replied Matt, "I mean he's got lot to think about, probably. He's, like, a bit more stressed about stuff, but he'll be OK." Matt had noticed Ravi *had* changed. Gone were the nights spent in with the Playstation and the geeky renditions of tunes off his iPod; instead he had gained an aura of quiet composure and a concern for his destiny. He did look worn, but it sort of suited him, thought Matt to himself.

"He should, like, get a bit more sleep," added Matt.

"Hmm," Ellie was not convinced that things were that simple. "What about you, Matt? How are you doing?"

"Me, I'm great. Couldn't be better. I'm in my element," said Matt. He wasn't being facetious, he really was enjoying applying his actually very logical mind to things. Appearances can be deceptive; behind the laid-back exterior, his mind was working overtime.

Bruce and Elspeth, being familiar with students and ex-students and their ways over a period of decades, had immediately recognised Matt's sincerity and willingness to help. They also quickly began to see that he had real ability too.

"OK, Matt. I believe you...although you could still do with a shave, you lazy bum!" Ellie threw a cushion towards him and Matt fell backwards, feigning injury. Right at that moment Ravi walked into the room.

"Is this a zoo or something?" he said picking up the cushion and throwing it back to Ellie.

"Lighten up, dude" Hard day or something?" Matt decided that he sometimes missed the old Ravi.

"Forget it, I'm sorry," said Ravi, rubbing his head with one hand, "I've just got a bit of a headache that's all."

"Hey, guys, lighten up," Ellie said, changing the subject, "Bruce contacted me just now and wants us to go online. He said he might have found something."

They gathered in front of the big screen and hooked up to the connection with the McLeish's in Edinburgh. Bruce's big, bearded face appeared, serious and inscrutable, filling the screen.

"Hello you young people," he boomed out of the wall.

"Hello Bruce," said Ellie, smiling towards the familiar image (she'd taken to calling her grand-parents by their first names, as an adult) "What's happening?...I got your message."

"Ah, yes...Well, before we get to that I just want to check on a few things. Now, Ravi, the picture of the Shaz did not have Doob in it did it...it wasn't cropped or anything like that to remove part of it?"

"No, that's the picture that Jammo sent me. I even went back and checked it with him and he said that that's what he got sent."

"Well, the thing is, one of the people that I know in the US sent me a picture this morning. I want to show you youngsters. Here it is"

Bruce's face disappeared and a few seconds later the screen was filled with a photo of a woman in her thirties, in some sort of work uniform, the kind of dark blue suit that an employee of a bank might wear. She was standing in what appeared to be an empty room apart from one other thing: standing next to her, unmistakably smiling, was another Shaz.

"Holy shit!" mouthed Matt, "It's one of the grey guys."

This time, the Shaz was definitely male looking. It stood almost nestling against the woman. The woman was looking at the Shaz with a look of unmistakable horror, the posture of her body indicating that she was trying to back away from it.

"She doesn't look too pleased to be there," said Ravi.

The three of them gazed at the screen, all now realising that this had become more than an isolated case.

"I wonder if there are any more," he added.

Bruce came back online. "I've sent that picture to you guys...but that's not all. The contact did not only get *one* picture. Shortly after sending that one he sent another. Here's that one."

Matt, Ravi and Ellie braced themselves for another shock. Once again the screen faded and a new image flashed up.

"It's the same woman!" exclaimed Ellie, "But she looks completely different.

It *was* the same woman but this time she was looking straight into the camera, not at the Shaz. Her grimace had gone and she looked as if she was smiling. She held the hand of the small squat figure beside her.

"That smile looks a bit forced." said Ravi, "Look at her eyes; that's not a real smile."

"That's what we thought, Ravi," Elspeth's voice appeared in the background. "That's what made us even more worried. I mean, the second picture is definitely staged to make it look like the woman is not that terrified...although who'd think that anyone would fall for it, I just don't know."

"Yes, it looks like the first picture was possibly sent in error, but it was too late to get it back, so whoever sent it sent another one off. Seems a very odd thing to do, but there you go." agreed Bruce.

"It seems a very frightening thing to do, " said Ravi, thinking of how terrified the woman had looked in the first picture; somehow, despite her smile, she looked even more terrified in the second picture. He thought about Doob's face in the video, it definitely had a similar look of veiled fear he thought. Doob just hid things better.

"Any clues about who she is?" asked Ellie, "She looks like she'd have work colleagues, people who might notice if she's gone missing."

"Yes, you're right, Ellie. We have got quite a lot as it happens," Bruce said, looking, as he would put it, 'a wee bit pleased with himself'.

"See her clothes, well obviously it's a uniform, and if you look at the jacket you can see that she's wearing a badge."

They stared at the lapel of the navy jacket.

"So we can tell where she works?" said Ellie.

"Better than that, Ellie. It's a *name* badge: we know exactly who she is!...You're looking at Victoria Romirez, a Brazilian regional government worker from Sao Paulo. She works for the regional economic development department and she's been reported missing for about two weeks."

"Has anyone seen the picture?" said Ravi.

"No, son. Our contact only got it himself yesterday—contacted me straight away. But he's sending the picture to the police, 'cos it's about a missing person. He'll make sure the picture could not be traced; otherwise he would have been in the frame for kidnapping himself!"

"That'll make things interesting."

"Might cause a bit of a stir, but I would brace yourself for the police saying that it is a hoax."

"Or some sort of twisted sicko," added Matt.

"Exactly."

Ravi felt something nagging away at him. The woman's name... Brazil; it all sounded familiar in some way but he couldn't put his finger on.

"Look," said Bruce, "I've sent you all the info and I'll keep you posted. I don't suppose this is the last of them somehow." Bruce paused and then presented his suggestion, "I'd like you folks to come and stay with us, up here in Edinburgh for a while. We've got all the facilities and video-calling is just not as good as thinking things over over a meal and a nice glass of whiskey now is it?...You *are* all over eighteen aren't you?

"Yes, Bruce, we are!" laughed Ellie "Well, that's very good of you. I think it's an excellent idea but we'll talk it through and let you know later. It's a group decision. OK?"

"Deal," said Bruce, "We'll hear from you later. Don't leave it too long; I've got a gut feeling that this is not going to be the last picture we get of a Shaz...or the last 'missing' person." The Mcleish's bid the group in London farewell and the screen flickered off.

Ravi, Matt and Ellie once again looked at each other, not as a group of flatmates but as a team—a team with an increasingly important purpose.

"I don't know about you, Matt, but I'm packing my bags as we speak."

For Ravi there was no real decision to be made: a part-time job in a mobile phone shop, or trying to saving his friend, people, potentially even the world, from whatever was happening. It really was a no-brainer.

"I hear you," replied Matt, "How we gonna get up there?"

Ravi pulled out his travelling suitcase from under his bad and flung it onto his bed. How different life seemed, compared to when he had last used the case a few short weeks ago. He felt like a different person: an older person. He started loading the case; not too many clothes but plenty of items to remind him of who he was: books, cards, little mementos he'd picked up along the way. He packed away the headphones that had been left for him (apparently) by Doob. He packed away the blue Goddess bracelet carefully, remembering it was another link to the Shaz and wondering what had become of the ragged little child who had sold it to him.

He opened a draw containing a random collection of papers from university and before: old essays, club flyers, administration, that sort of thing. He moved the papers around a bit and then decided to tip the whole drawer out onto the bed—that way he could just throw anything he didn't want out. Rifling through the pile of stuff, he picked a few bits out, reading the odd line and mostly consigning whatever it was to the bin. He saved the odd item and put them in a separate pile to take to Edinburgh. He pulled out an old stapled booklet; poor quality, like it had been printed on an ink-jet, the colours slightly off. That's when he realised where he recognised the name of the woman on the photograph from.

The booklet was an assignment he remembered doing at school for a business studies assignment. Something to do with emerging markets and economic growth. He remembered that people in his team contacted places in different 'BRIC' countries to show how economies were dominating growth in specific sectors. His area was Brazil, more specifically Sao Paolo. He looked at the list of credits at the back of the booklet, the people who had helped the students by supplying local information by email. Under 'Brazil' were three names: the last one was Victoria Romerez.

TO EDINBURGH

It was now clear to Ravi that, so far, *he* was the common element linking the cases together: he was Doob's friend, he had contacted Victoria Romerez, he had seen the un-named little girl disappear. Of course, the clearest indication that he was central to the whole story was the fact that the Shaz had *told* Ellie that he was who they were looking for.

"Do you think I'm gonna end up with *them*?" he'd asked Ellie on the train up to Edinburgh.

"I don't know, Ravi, " she'd replied, hoping inside that this would not be the case. "I guess we all could."

Ravi turned his head and watched the northern countryside rolling by; the journey reminded him of the chugging diesel train ride all those years ago in Chamba. I'm ready for my destiny, he thought to himself.

Bruce and Elspeth, had of course, come to meet them at Edinburgh Waverley Station and waved enthusiastically at them as they passed though the barriers.

"Welcome one and all," said Bruce, "Welcome to Scotland."

They packed all of their cases and bags into the back of Bruce's Land-Rover (he still liked the old workhorse—though it was a different one to the one they had travelled in fifteen years ago) and all got into the vehicle. On the way to Juniper Green, Bruce and Elspeth pointed out a few sights of the city: Princes Street, The Mound, The Castle, Redford Barracks and so on. Ravi and Matt marvelled at the elegant gothic-styled architecture and long, stylish stone-laid streets. It all looked so clean and beautifully designed. Despite the car being full of comment and 'getting to know you' talk, all of them were waiting for the real conversation to start.

After the guests had been shown to their rooms, everyone gathered in the dining room for dinner. The McLeish's lived in a very old and rather regal house with large rooms, stuffed full of an interesting assortment of comfortable old furniture and old curios, Ravi could see why Ellie had loved growing up there.

"Can you think of any reason whatsoever why you would be of interest to the Shaz?" Elspeth asked Ravi, "Anything at all...I mean why choose you over other people?"

Ravi could not give a reason. He was just a regular young guy, trying to get his life together and realising that life was not as easy as he had imagined it being when he was younger.

"Something possibly to do with my heritage..." he said weakly, unconvinced by his own suggestion, "Could be to do with an ancient link to something to do with India?"

No-one seemed to buy this, although nothing was 'off the table' so to speak. Talk seemed to go round and round in circles. No-one seemed to know very much more than when they had last spoken over the video-call. The police in Sao Paolo were now looking for a kidnap gang with a 'weird imagination' and that was about it. Ellie had sent a message to domino236ot but nothing had come back in return. The evening was spent with everyone going down to Elspeth's lab and looking at images of the ghoulish finger. Matt spent several hours studying slides and reports with Elspeth whilst Ravi looked at press articles about missing people; Bruce questioning him about whether any of the people in the articles might have some link to his life. They did not.

God, I hope this isn't a waste of time, thought Ravi.

A couple of days passed with no developments. Ellie decided that, rather than being stuck in the house all the time, she would take Ravi and Matt into some of her old student haunts in town, so they headed for the University and then walking out through The

Meadows to Bruntsfield for a coffee.

"D'you like it here, guys?" Ellie knew that Ravi and Matt would be bewitched by the elegant, wide Victorian streets; the tall rows of buildings housing quaint and trendy independent shops at ground level, peeling off into side roads comprising uniform terraces of historic proportion and style.

"I could cope," said Ravi, "I suppose I could just about put up with the cold."

"Lightweight!" replied Ellie, "What about you, Matt?"

Matt didn't reply, he was too busy looking out of the window of the café. There was someone there, on the other side of the road, perhaps a child waiting at the bus-stop he thought. Someone or *something* looking in their direction. People could be quite pale in Scotland but this person looked decidedly *grey*. Scarf wrapped closely round, possibly to hide something...and glasses that dark, in winter? Then again, he thought, it could have been an old lady with a visual impairment; maybe he was just being paranoid. Then again...

"Look, over there," he said urgently, turning back to the others and then pointing frantically to the person, "isn't that one of them?"

"Where?" said Ravi, desperately looking through the shop-front up and down the hill.

A bus drove away on the opposite side, leaving an empty bus stop.

"Oh, no matter, dude. I just thought I saw something, it was probably nothing though. Just someone waiting for a bus." They were all a bit on edge and he had not had a good night's sleep—his mind was probably playing tricks on him. He looked out of the window again...there in the shop doorway opposite was...

"Quick, it's one of them!" he called, grabbing his coat and

darting for the door. The other followed.

"Well, that was embarrassing," said Matt when they got back to the big house..."Sorry, guys."

"Yeah, especially when the owner of the café thought we'd done a runner to avoid paying," said Ellie, rather annoyed that it had happened on her 'home turf'.

"Don't worry about it Matt, seeing a kid in the shadows: anyone could have made that mistake."

Matt looked down at the floor, sullenly.

"Hey, dude. You did the right thing—thanks," Ravi continued warmly and meaning what he said. "Thanks, for being here, bro— it means a lot."

"Is that you kids out there?" Bruce called from the other room. "You better come in here; something's happened."

It was more than 'something' it was a number of things. Whilst the trio had been out having coffee in the city Bruce had been checking out the latest from the gradually more and more interested network round the globe. There had been *two* more pictures and a video.

The pictures all had similar but slightly different formats. In each of them a person was standing next to a Shaz. In the first picture the apparently teenage girl was carrying a book, although the title was obscured by her hand, she was accompanied by a female Shaz. In the second picture a man, dressed in sports gear of some kind was next to a male Shaz.

"I know that guy," Ravi said, a mixture of sorrow and excitement in his voice, "That's my old maths teacher from school: Mr Tranter."

"Good, that should save us a bit of time," commented Elspeth, "But we've got more to show you."

"Notice how each of the creatures looks slightly different, said Bruce, "They are all individuals, just like we are."

"Well, not *just* like we are," interjected Elspeth, "But you understand what we are saying."

The faces of the two people in the pictures had the same strained look and forced smile of the previous picture and video. The people in the pictures were scared.

"Now we come to the big one," said Bruce, "The video."

The video was very different to the other one featuring Doob. In an empty white room was a Shaz, his broad face clearly expressing something, although it was difficult to put one's finger on the exact emotion: annoyance perhaps, or discomfort; perhaps that was just the way a Shaz looked? He started to talk.

"Ravi, we are glad you have found us. We have prepared with your guidance and friends of friends have assisted us, also. You must keep to the rules and involve no outsiders"

That was all. The video flickered off. The Shaz had a sort of pseudo-imposing air about him thought Ravi, very disconcerting. He had no idea what they were talking about.

"Well, Ravi. There it is; these 'things' are clearly in control and they are now seemingly taking people willy-nilly off the streets."

"Why are they choosing those people and how can we stop them?" said Bruce, half to himself. "Look we have to get a move on now, this is escalating. Today its two people, tomorrow it could be ten...who knows." He looked at Ravi, "Who's the girl?"

"I've got no idea!" said Ravi glumly.

"Right well, there's our first task. If we can work out who these Shaz creatures are taking, perhaps we can work out why and warn people. We might need to open this up...God knows what the reaction's going to be!"

"Hold on a minute...can we blow up the book she's got her hand on?" asked Ravi.

"Sure," said Bruce clicking on his laptop a couple of times. "I couldn't make it out though."

"I know what it is, I know what it is!!" Ravi couldn't believe it, "I recognise the design...It's the 'Two Towers': the second book from the 'Lord of the Rings'. I *gave* that book to a friend of mine when I left sixth-form: Mark Wooley."

"Right, let's check to see if anyone connected to your friend Mark has gone missing in the past few days. Have you still got his details Ravi? You could give him a call. No, wait, that's not a good idea: people might get the wrong end of the stick. Let me put the word around instead."

"Look, Sir. I've somehow unwittingly got people into this mess and I think I should be getting people out of it," Ravi said, without a hint of self-importance. "Do you think I should offer to exchange places with those people."

"Well, that's very generous of you, son, but no, I don't. Firstly, if they wanted you to do that I think they would have told us themselves, or they would have taken you in the first place and secondly," he paused and looked at Ellie, "Secondly, who's going to go out with my wee grand-daughter there." Bruce looked over at Ravi and winked, knowingly.

"Bruce" Ellie exclaimed, "Stop joking around." She had turned a deep shade of pink and mumbled to Ravi that her grand-dad was always embarrassing her like that, before scurrying out of the room.

Bruce laughed heartily. "So, none of this swapping places malarky then?" he said, turning back to Ravi, "That stuffs just on films anyway...and of course you haven't got us into anything. *We* got *you* into it, remember?"

Ravi thought about it and could hardly argue with Bruce, after all, if Ellie had not gone down to London and found him, he would be unlikely to be here now.

"OK, Sir, look lets get a plan together. Otherwise we'll just be going round in circles. This is serious. What if they take my mother or my brother—or you or Ellie? We have to stop this and get those people back"

"Atta-boy, that's the idea...now someone call Ellie back, we've all got work to do."

Ellie gave Bruce a withering look when she came back into the room, but after that she returned to being as composed and professional as ever.

Together they spent the rest of the evening getting the basic facts straight and some idea of what they were each going to do. This is what they scrawled up on the old chalk board in Bruce's study:

- People that had seemingly had some connection to Ravi were somehow being lured away or otherwise abducted by aliens.

- The aliens may have some help in the guise of some person or persons (thus far in the guise of a man who appeared to be of eastern European origin);

- Images of at least some of the victims had been openly shared with them;

- The victims looked scared;

- No ransom or demands had been made;

- There was no indication as to where the victims were, what was to become of them, or how many had or would be taken.

There was an awful lot of uncertainty, thought Ravi and no

indication of how to stop the débâcle. "Should we go to the police anyway?" he asked his companions, "I kinda feel we should."

"The guy said no outside involvement, remember dude?" Matt reminded him, "What if you tell the law and it just pisses the Shaz off...think what they'll do then"

"Good point," said Ellie, "My vote's against it, let's see what we can do first. After all they haven't *harmed* anyone yet."

Ravi thought of the the faces of the captured people and the fear in Doob's voice. He was not that convinced. Then again, what exactly were the police going to *do*, or indeed MI5 or the CIA?

"OK, we go it alone, for now. In that case, we need to do three things: find out why this is happening, stop any more abductions and get the people with the Shaz out...once we find out where they are."

"Great plan, my boy," agreed Bruce, "We need to get to those things...find out where they are and what they want."

"Ellie, you've got a point of direct contact with domino236ot and I can try them myself using the coolio345londonboy tag. Let's do that tonight," suggested Ravi

"As far as we know, no-one has managed to get any further with contacting the 'Shaz', as we're calling them, but we can press for more help," Bruce said, "We also need to be alert for any further abductions."

"I think that Matt and I should redouble our efforts to work out their physiology. After all, if things get nasty it might be helpful to know what their weak spots are. We also need to work out the way they think and to do that we really need more contact; so far we have quite limited information but we'll make a start," Elspeth added. Finding a way to negotiate with the Shaz would need more than just locating them.

"Matt, how about we put our heads together and see if we can work out how these guys think...bit of psychological profiling, as it were?"

"Perfect, " replied Matt. "By the way, the others haven't said anything, but I *did* see one of them today, you know. I'm certain. I didn't imagine it...Like, it was different to the kid in the doorway, guys. When the bus passed, that's when I lost track of it."

Bruce and Elspeth looked at each other, knowingly and then back at Matt.

"We believe you, son," said Bruce quietly, "We haven't said anything to Ellie but over the years we've spotted them, occasionally. Now I know we're getting old but we're not quite senile yet!"

"OK—Well maybe they sort of *live* somewhere round here; they've got their space-ship moored up locally or something. Anything's worth a shot," said Ravi. " You said that they talked to you not too far away, all those years ago, maybe we should go back and have a look around for any clues."

"We've been back plenty of times. Found absolutely nothing," realising he sounded discouraging, Bruce added, "but that doesn't mean that there's nothing there; or they might want to meet us there again. I know the co-ordinates."

The five of them knew that they were involved in something that they were compelled to continue with: it was their destiny to resolve whatever it was that was happening. For Bruce and Elspeth it really was an opportunity to use the knowledge they had collected over the decades and for Matt, Ravi and Ellie this was the experience that was going to shape the rest of their lives.

"Well, I've got to rest," sighed Ravi, looking drained. Tomorrow, let's try and find out the state of play with the girl and Mr Tranter and see if we can find out why this is happening."

The group peeled off to their own rooms for the night. Ravi

tried to sleep a little but his thoughts haunted him, so he got up and switched on his notebook. There must be something here, he thought as he scrolled through sites looking for clues; the four people that had been 'taken' seemed to have very ordinary seeming lives, without anything linking them apart from him. But *why* him?

He searched through sites looking for 'alien' stories about people that had been abducted and then returned. Bruce had sent him links to the most promising examples, scattered all over the world. Ravi found little similarity to their situation; people seemed to have been taken and then just returned (sometimes having been through 'experiments')—no pictures were sent of them. Ravi concluded that some of the 'victims' were probably sexual fantasists, and the rest were not going to be of much help. There was no point in wasting time.

Ravi sent out messages as coolio345londonboy via the site that Ellie had been speaking to the Shaz on and also posted a general message to all the social networking sites he could think of, saying that coolio345londonboy wanted to talk to domino236ot and sort things out. I hope I don't get too many crank replies, he thought. He was confident that anything genuine would be clearly identified.

He must have fallen asleep at some point.

WE MEET AGAIN

The next day dawned bright and crisp over Edinburgh. Ravi had woken up at his computer and continued surfing for anything that might be useful. Going to the local news page for London he saw that a local teenager—Sarah Wooley, aged fifteen, from Blackheath, had gone missing and police were appealing for any help. At least that's saved us some time, thought Ravi. He was half tempted to pick up the phone to the Metropolitan Police but remembered the decision. "No police," he said out loud to himself. He could find nothing on Mr Tranter, but he was sure that it would only be a matter of time.

The team decided to part company for the day; Bruce would continue to research from the house and monitor for any new developments. Matt and Elspeth were going to carry on trying to find out what the Shaz *were* exactly and what made them tick. Ravi and Ellie were going to go back to the site near Bonnybridge where the Shaz had appeared all those years ago.

"I'll drive us," Ellie had said when Ravi asked how they were going to get there.

"You *drive*?" Ravi had said. In London no-one he knew seemed to have a car. It just didn't make sense, both because of the nightmarish ordeal of actually driving in seemingly perpetual traffic jams and because it was so damn expensive to run a car. Using the tube and bus was second nature to most Londoners.

"Of course I drive! It's more difficult to get around without knowing how to drive up here," explained Ellie curtly, "If you live in the middle of nowhere, it's the only real option for many of us Scots. I guess you wouldn't say that Edinburgh's the middle of nowhere but Bruce taught me when I was seventeen, so that I could go to the forests for star-gazing and get about to see folk away from the city."

Ellie was a bit annoyed with herself for sounding defensive (and she realised that actually she probably could get around just as well using public transport) and Ravi was annoyed with himself for questioning the fact that she could drive. She probably thinks I'm some sort of bigot, who thinks that only men should have cars, he thought to himself.

"Look, I didn't mean..." he started to apologise.

"Sorry I snapped at you!" Ellie said at the same time.

They both laughed.

"Just get in the car," said Ellie, crunching over the gravel to the to the old, brown Ford Fiesta parked at the side of the garage, "Unless you want to go by bike?"

Ellie and Ravi made their way through the countryside further to the west of Edinburgh, passing through the open landscape, dotted with greyish hills and leafy coppices. Sheep were scattered in the fields to the side of the road and small, well-to-do settlements flitted past at regular intervals. It must have been a wonderful place to grow up, thought Ravi.

Conversation between them in the car was spartan and focused. Ravi wanted to know whether there was anything that she knew that she had not let on about, after all it had been Ellie that had come down to seek him out; before she had arrived he was just living a normal kind of life. It was she that had had previous contact with the Shaz, rather than choosing him they seemed to have chosen her first, he thought to himself.

For her part, Ellie asked Ravi what it was that might link the victims, other than him. Did they know each other?—only by association with him, he replied. Did he have any special knowledge, skills or 'powers' that might have attracted the Shaz to him?—definitely not, as far as he knew, replied Ravi. Like most people of their age, Ravi did think of himself as perhaps being a little bit more talented than he actually was, but he was grounded enough to realise that he was not going to change the world; at least not until very recently and possibly for reasons that he did not understand.

Ravi kept checking his phone for any texts from back at the house, or for replies to the messages that he had sent out to the Shaz, but since reception was quite intermittent he couldn't really pick anything up.

"You got a signal, Ellie?" he asked in desperation, "I can't get any bars."

"What?...Oh, yeah, sorry I was miles away. Yeah you have to choose the right network round here. D'you want to use my internet."

"It's OK," decided Ravi, "I'm just getting obsessed!"

"OK then, well we're not that far now anyway. This is the side road we turned down, seems to go out to the middle of nowhere doesn't it?"

She turned down a narrow road, bordered by a stone wall on either side. "You know there are quite a few sightings of UFOs near Bonnybridge? We thought maybe it's on a ley line or something like that, none of them have been like ours though, and non of them have led to people being 'taken'."

A few miles further on and they stopped. The car sat, a lonely brown shape on the empty, grey ribbon of road. Everything had a grey-green cast to it in the late autumn gloom. Sound seemed to have disappeared to a large extent, the overwhelming quality to the landscape was emptiness. You could see why it would have been a good place from which to spot stars.

"Right, out of the car," Ellie said purposefully, breaking the spell, "I'll show you exactly where it all happened."

The car had stopped near the only small landmark, the same landmark that Bruce had used to gauge where to park fifteen years ago; there was a fluorescent road sign on the side with a red triangle warning of the 'sharp bend ahead'. Ellie walked past it to a gap in the wall.

"This is where I hid behind the wall to go to the loo," she said indicating the gap. "Elspeth was here and Bruce was over there," she said gesturing with her hand. "That means the space-ship must have been round about here," she said, pacing over to where the craft had balanced on the wall. "I don't really know what we are supposed to be looking for."

"Nothing in particular," said Ravi, "Just see if anything comes to mind, or jumps out at us...not literally, I mean."

"Ha, ha," Ellie said, "You're quite the joker, aren't you Rav?"

After a while they decided to walk down the road a little, just to do something different.

"Do you get the feeling that we are being *watched*," said Ravi, a little nervously.

"Watched? no, you're just not used to the countryside—Londonboy."

However, Ellie did have a feeling that they weren't quite alone. Something was making the hairs on the back of her neck tingle.

"This is far enough," she said, "We better be heading back soon: it'll be getting dark in a couple of hours and we shouldn't be too late back."

They started walking back along along the road to the car, not saying anything. The air was cold and still. Ravi could hear his own breathing and the thudding of their boots against the tarmac. His mind drifted to the previous evening; he wondered whether

Bruce had meant what he said about Ellie going out with him? It was probably just a joke, he thought to himself: she's well out of my league. Then again, *something* had thrown them together, maybe there was hope after all?

Ravi was still thinking through the possible permutations of meaning surrounding himself and Ellie being thrown together, when he realised that Ellie's footsteps were no longer thudding in time with his own. She was no longer walking next to him. Oh, my God, she's been taken, he thought with a start. He swung around frantically and was relieved to see her familiar figure a few metres away. Ellie had stopped and was staring up the road, when she saw Ravi looking at her she scampered forward to catch up, pointing at the brown car in the near distance.

"Look, can you see it?" she hissed at Ravi, continuing to point at the car.

Ravi peered into the gloom that had started to set in, all he could see was the old brown Ford Fiesta.

"There, there!" Ellie directed his gaze towards the driver side door. There was a small crouched figure, looking in their direction. It turned and then turned back again.

"Quick, quick, before it gets away. This is amazing. Come ON, Ravi."

Ellie had started running towards the car, Ravi ran after her, slightly less enthusiastically. Perhaps a more cautious approach would have been better, he thought to himself.

They stopped about fifteen feet from the car and looked at the creature. It was definitely a Shaz. It looked at them silently with a long, lingering stare.

"Say something to it," urged Ellie.

"Hello, I'm Ravi...The one you seek...you know coolio345londonboy," Ravi thought he sounded like an idiot. Then he remembered Doob and the others and what this was really all about.

"I don't know what's going on, but we want you to release all the people that you have taken: Doob, Victoria Romerez, Mr Tranter, Sarah Wolley, the little Indian kid...and any more that you might have stashed away," Ravi said, purposefully. "Those people have friends and families who are missing them. Please, tell me what you want, perhaps we can work something out?"

"Well done," whispered Ellie, "That sounded good."

The Shaz just stood and looked at them. Then it started to speak.

"Coolio345londonboy, it is good to meet you. Your friends are not as good as we thought they would be. We are growing tired of them."

"What the hell do you mean...?" said Ravi, "Let them go then, PLEASE let them go and just go home."

"We don't want to!"

"What?" said Ravi, "What sort of an answer is that!"

"Coolio345londonboy—Ravi as you call yourself, we just want a bit more time. We'll give your friends back, we promise." The Shaz turned around as if looking for someone again, "We gave you a clue didn't we? One of us gave you her finger. That is more than fair."

"A clue to what?" Ellie asked, "Who are you?"

"Too many questions, too many questions..." said the Shaz, holding his large head in his little, stumpy hands. "I can't tell you who we are, I don't want to get into trouble...besides you have given us a name, Ravi, you can continue calling us by the name you have chosen'."

"But what do you call yourselves?" asked Ravi, "What are

you...what is your kind called?"

"I have to go now," said the Shaz, suddenly looking a bit guilty. He shuffled out of view behind the car. Ravi thought he could hear strange, croaky whispering. Then, out of no-where appeared a domed, saucer-shaped space-ship, identical in design to the one that Ellie had seen when she was a child. It swooped down and paused for a few seconds, two Shaz bounced up from behind the car and into the small windowed door space. Then the craft moved off again, its grey shape camouflaged against the darkening skyline and quickly disappeared.

"Well, what do you make of THAT?" Ellie asked after a few minutes gazing into the sky looking after the space craft. "I wish, I'd remembered to press record on my mobile. I can't remember what he said, exactly...It all seemed so confused."

"He said something about being bored of the people they had captured...or something like that. He also said that they *promised* to let people go."

"But then they said that they didn't want to," Ellie reminded him.

"Yeah, to be quite honest it was all a bit weird...The way he spoke, something about not wanting to get into trouble. It was really cryptic."

"Totally doolally as far as I can tell, and that makes them potentially very dangerous," warned Ellie.

"He said they wanted more time, time for *what*? They gave us a clue, about *what*?"

Talking to the Shaz had been like trying to talk to a shifty east Londoner trading out of the back of a suitcase. It had left Ravi with no real answers, but there *were* some things to go on: the finger was a clue (had Elspeth and Matt found out anything new? he wondered); they were taking people for some *reason*—perhaps to perform some task. They also seemed quite touchy, he thought: very over-sensitive.

"He certainly didn't seem evil," said Ellie, "He seemed quite ridiculous, if anything."

"Appearances can be deceptive, Ellie. Don't forget that they've got several people captive before you start saying how cute they are."

"Hey, Good point Ravi, sorry."

"No sweat. Now, lets get back and tell the others about this conversation," Ravi looked anxiously at Ellie, "Do you think I handled it OK?" Ravi felt the pressure of talking to aliens was beginning to take its toll on him.

"You did great Ravi! Look we are here to back each other up right?"

"Right," said Ravi, inside however he could feel his inner voice crying out for an easy life in the noisy but predictable company of his Sony Playstation.

Back at the house, the news of Ravi and Ellie's encounter was listened to with sombre attention in the study. Bruce asked Ravi to write down the exact conversation, as he and Ellie remembered it, on any empty space on the chalkboard. They asked questions about the way that the Shaz had sounded, how it had looked and so on. Elspeth was particularly interested and intrigued by some of the elements that had made no sense to Ravi: features such as the guilty demeanour of the Shaz and the fact that it didn't want to get into trouble.

"He may have broken ranks with the rest of his kind," she said, speculating, "Or it could have been a lower-order member of the community."

"We've been examining the finger samples again guys and it's, like, not telling us anything new. It is definitely organic, similar to our physiology but with some differences in chemical composition and some structures that we haven't been able to work out, " said Matt.

"We've sent samples out to labs in Switzerland and Ireland and we're expecting the results in a week or two," added Elspeth.

One of the main developments had been the leak of Bruce's involvement in a new 'project' involving possible extra-terrestrials to the press. So far it was relatively low key; Bruce had been careful to keep the details of the events a secret to all but those he trusted deeply. Nevertheless, any breach of the details could have serious repercussions for the outcome. In addition, Bruce did not want to conjure up any interest from the vast community of ill-informed sceptics *or* ardent ET worshippers. Retirement was meant to equal a quieter life, in his case it had amounted to anything but!

"What about news on any of the missing people?" asked Ravi, vaguely hoping that one of them had miraculously re-appeared with some mad-cap story about being captured by aliens, but otherwise alive and well.

"Nothing, none of the people has turned up. The disappearances, in the case of the latest victims are being taken very seriously, especially that of the young girl—Sarah," Bruce's voice was solemn. "There's more," he added, ominously, "I've been scouring local sources to see whether there have been any unusual reports of people going missing: unexpected, out of character, that sort of thing. I've made a list of these people and I'd like you, Ravi, to look through it and tell me if you recognise any of the names, workplaces or establishments, even locations, that they are linked with. Check their names against your social media networks—this 'friends' business sounds very Facebook to me"

Yeah, totally agree," said Matt, "You're on those sites, like, *a lot* bro!...or at least you used to be"

It was true that Ravi had spent a fair proportion of his spare time (and a significant proportion of his 'not spare' time) on social media networks. He thought of the hundreds, if not thousands of fans, followers and other links he must have made over the years.

As if reading his thoughts Bruce announced the next thing he had been organising.

"With Ellie's help I've managed to get a list together of all your Facebook, Linkedin and Twitter friends and followers and all your phone contacts including those that you deleted. That has not been easy, let me tell you. I have *not* been able to get any other networks mapped out—say from your school days. You'll have to help us with that. We are still working on a list of anything you commented on, on any of the networks. The good thing is, when we have all of these details plotted out for all the missing people on the list, it should be easy to see if there are any matches.

The bad news is that it could include half of England, thought Ravi, sorrowfully. "Have we received any images?" he asked, "That might make it easier to identify people."

"No, not yet...and it could be that all of these people have nothing to do with Ravi, and the Shaz have nothing to do with them going missing; lets hope that they're not even really missing. But I think it's better to start being pro-active now, we can't just sit back and wait for things to happen. We need to see if there is any pattern to this thing."

"Agreed," said Ravi, emphatically. He knew that it was not going to be easy. What really worried him was the fact that, given the range of possible links that Bruce had described, a *very* high number of people could become potential victims. You don't really stop and think how many people you might have a vague connection to, he thought to himself.

Ellie had been quiet since they had got back to the house. She was feeling tired and needed to rest so that she could get her brain into gear. She was annoyed with herself for seeing the Shaz as a rather pathetic creature and forgetting the lives that were being destroyed by their actions. Ellie knew not to be taken in by people playing the sympathy card until she really knew their story. Still, if she could only get some more time with the Shaz, surely she would be able to understand their motives?

Ravi realised that he hadn't checked his phone all day: he'd given up when he couldn't get a signal on the road out towards Bonnybridge. He pulled it out of his pocket. That's odd, he thought, six missed calls and he didn't recognise the number. He pressed return call and waited—it went straight to voicemail.

"Hey, Ellie, fancy finding out who owns this number? I'm sure your mates won't find it hard," he forwarded the number on to her phone.

"No problem, Ravi. Just leave it with me."

RUMOURS

Looking at Bruce's spreadsheets, showing all of his social media contacts and ex-contacts, Ravi wondered just how on earth he had managed to accrue such a large number of 'friends' of just a few years. I don't even know who these people are, he thought to himself, why on earth did I agree to accept them as contacts? The task that he had been set by Bruce - to try to get together a list of links made through other sites and informal online groups, was proving impossible. If Ravi couldn't even remember most of the people on the sites he *did* know about, how on earth was he going to uncover any details for sites he didn't have a clue about? He decided to concentrate on looking through the list of people that had gone missing recently and see whether any names looked familiar.

Bruce had set out the list by date, covering the past fortnight only and confined to the UK. The abductions could have stretched further back in time, but he thought that it was far more likely, since part of the process seemed to be to get the message to Ravi, that the Shaz had only recently started 'kidnapping' people. Despite the fact that the list only covered a couple of weeks it already had thousands of names on it. The list was being added to day by day.

Ravi had no idea that so many went missing every day; details of people from eight to eighty were laid out before him. People from all walks of life, from doctors to students and from businessmen to unemployed people. Some of the names had brief stories attached, outlining what had happened: Shany Williams, a waitress from Wrexham had gone out to take the dog for a walk and the dog had come back alone; David Coates had disappeared just days after being awarded a major engineering prize; Mustapha Mirza went missing, leaving his heavily pregnant wife and young child. The list seemed full of individual mini-stories of personal angst and mystery. Despite his best efforts, Ravi found himself drawn into thinking about what could have made people just walk out one day, potentially never to see again all of the people who had populated their lives to that point. At least they made the decision themselves, he thought, remembering that Doob and the others had not had that luxury.

None of the names on the list seemed to be people he knew personally, although it was difficult to be certain, given that Ravi did not exactly know the names of all the people he interacted with. There were pictures attached to most of the names, but he didn't notice any faces that he knew. Almost any of them could, for example, have been customers in the phone shop where he worked, or he could have been talking to them in a pub and he would never have known. However, since they were, for now at least, looking for directly known and recognised contacts, he could not really see any on the first few pages. He had many pages to go.

I've brought you a cup of tea to keep you going," Ellie said, trying to be encouraging, "Any luck?"

"Not so far, but hey, I've only got about twenty pages to go through! Any news on that mobile number?"

"Oh, yeah. That's what I've come in to tell you, it's a pay-as-you-go, I'm afraid, virtually untraceable; the best bet is probably to keep calling it, or whoever it is might try to call you back."

Ravi didn't hold out too much hope, he'd been trying the number intermittently and it always went straight to voicemail. It's probably in a ditch somewhere with no battery, he thought. He went back to looking though the list, ploughing carefully through, not daring to overlook one single name, in case it was linked to him. The task was going to take more than one day, and, by tomorrow, God knows how many more people would be added, perhaps the best bet would be to wait for the Shaz to contact them again. He decided to go outside, just into the McLeish's garden for some cool evening air to clear his head.

Bruce and Elspeth had spent the day in town, leaving their young guests to get on with the different tasks back in the house. "Not everyone wants us oldies around all the time...let's get out of their hair for a wee while," Elspeth had suggested. Bruce thought it was a great plan, especially since he had wanted to talk to his wife about something in private.

He wanted to talk about a phone call he had received from an insider in a US intelligence agency. The call was pretty low key, just a catch up really, according to the agent. Bruce knew that his interest in extra-terrestrials was noted by governments around the world—these things always are. They wanted to protect their information and prevent anything happening that might cause them embarrassment, for example by contradicting anything that *they* were putting out there. Most of all, they wanted to be the first (and hopefully only) people to know if there was anything at all that might have an impact on national or global SETUrity. The abduction of innocent people by the Shaz definitely fitted into this category.

Word had obviously got out via his network to the Agency concerned. Bruce trusted his contacts, but it was almost inevitable that someone would make a careless comment, perhaps to a research student they were supervising, which might then be mentioned over coffee with a group of people and so on, till it reached someone that would want to have a chat with Bruce.

The agent knew about the existence of a photo that showed one of the Shaz with a person. Since the person was described as a woman Bruce knew it was Victoria Romerez (the other female victim in a picture was Sarah Wooley who would most likely have been described as a girl). This made sense, of course; the Agent didn't say that he knew that the person in the picture *was* Victoria Romerez but, if he did, he would know that Victoria was Brazilian. South American political allegiances were of great importance to the United States. The agent wanted to keep things low key; the picture was most likely a hoax (he knows its not, Bruce thought to himself as he held the phone to his ear) and they were trying to find out where it originated from. It would be good to work as a team with Bruce, the agent said; would Bruce please let them know if he made any progress with the picture. Of course he would, said Bruce...just as soon as he heard anything.

"Lets hope the floodgates don't open then," said Elspeth, pouring out some coffee as they sat in 'Josie's Roast', one of their favourite coffee shops in Edinburgh, squeezing into an alcove near the back of the shop so that they wouldn't be disturbed.

"If we can stop things in their tracks we might be OK, Elspeth, but if things get any worse I think we'll have their big muddy boots all over our carpet!" Bruce grumbled. "Mind you, if things get any worse, we might be glad to have them around."

"I can tell you now, from what Matt and I have deduced about the Shaz, that they are not going to take kindly to the sort of macho approach that you and I know that those boys would probably come over with," sighed Elspeth, "Then there's the way they would 'deal with' Ravi if they ever found out that the Shaz were focusing their attention on people connected with him. The poor wee thing would become a prisoner, or worse than that..."

"Some sort of bait, perhaps?" said Bruce, "Someone to lure them in."

"Aye."

It didn't bear thinking about and the couple mulled over the situation for some time, reaching no conclusion.

"Well, I suppose we'd best be getting back home, old girl,"

Bruce said eventually, twisting round to get his coat, "Oh...no..."

"What is it?"

"Look, over there, NO, don't look. Oh, its too late: he's coming over."

A balding, spectacled, middle-aged man wearing a shapeless, olive-green jacket and jeans was trying to manoeuvre his way through the tiny café towards them, waving the folded newspaper he was carrying towards them occasionally as he went. Bruce looked as if he would have liked to have crawled under the table to hide but, instead, acknowledged the approaching man with a slight raise of his hand.

"It's Frank Tobin, that irritating journalist from the Bonnybridge Herald," Bruce said to Elspeth through the corner of his mouth, "He's a right pain in the backside!...Special interest in UFOs."

Frank puffed his way to their table and held out a sweaty hand to Bruce as he arrived. "Bruce, good to see you again—Frank, Frank Tobin, Bonnybridge Herald, mind if I sit down and join you for a wee while?"

"Well, actually Frank, we were just going...we've really got to get back."

Frank ignored Elspeth and pulled over a chair.

"So Bruce, long time no see! Last time I seen you was when I was doing that UFO story about the woman from Falkirk and the lights she seen over the Water of Leith."

"She was drunk," said Bruce, sharply, "The lady admitted that she'd made up the story under the influence of two litres of White Lightening cider, for a laugh."

"Well, that's as may be, but you'll know, being our own genuine *celebrity* (he said the word slowly to emphasise the point) that Bonnybridge is the site of a fair few visitations by our extra-terrestrial friends," Frank smoothed his hair down, "Is this your good lady wife?"

"Yes, it is Frank, now what do you want?...because we want to leave." Indeed Bruce was considering the direct approach of just leaving.

"Now don't you worry...I won't keep you both, but a while. The thing is, Bruce, I've heard that you and your lovely wee grand-daughter have been visited by one of *them* and that they've made personal contact with you. My sources say that this 'encounter' happened in Falkirk county. Local people would be very interested in the details, Bruce... Now, can you give me any quotes at all? When it happened? What they said to you? Did they make any demands? Could they speak English, or did you communicate with them in some other way?...that sort of thing.." Frank paused and looked at Bruce expectantly. Bruce said nothing, he wanted to see just how much Frank knew before speaking.

" I have heard something else about people being *kidnapped*. Aye, *kidnapped* by aliens, right here in Bonnybridge. What do say to that, Mr McLeish." Frank had taken a small reporter's notebook from his jacket pocket and had a pencil poised to start writing.

"The answer to your question is no, I cannot give you a quote, unless you count 'No Comment'" said Bruce emphatically, "Furthermore, I don't know who these 'sources' are but what you're saying is, frankly, a load of baloney, as they say in New York; I suggest that you get yourself some new sources."

Bruce stood up and started putting on his coat. "Come on Elspeth, we're going home."

The couple marched purposefully out of the shop , towards their parked Land-Rover.

"Well, you certainly showed him what was what!" said Elspeth as they got to the vehicle, "Typical of the press; just can't get rid of them. Well, at least he's got the message."

Bruce was more concerned. Although he had got some details wrong, Frank Tobin did seem to have some accurate information about the Shaz from somewhere...but where? He was a local reporter but, once one hack (even one as low down the pecking order as Frank) started sniffing around, then others would follow. Also, Frank might be a rubbish reporter but his personal interest in UFOs and extra-terrestrials meant that he wouldn't just drop the story: he would be back.

"First the agent from America calling and now this, Elspeth," he said turning on the ignition, "This feels terribly like it's going to break into the open doesn't it?"

"And if it does, then the lives of those poor folk might be at risk...remember they said specifically that others should not be involved. We don't know what they might do."

"You're right, Elle, but I've got a terrible feeling that the whole thing is going to be taken out of our hands by events."

Elspeth was thinking once again about her perception of the Shaz. She did not think that they would take kindly to their instructions being ignored: 'highly volatile and unpredictable', that was their assessment when she and Matt had analysed their behaviour thus far—likely to escalate behaviour if stressed or annoyed. She hoped that Frank would keep his mouth shut for a while.

HOW MANY?

It had taken a couple of days, but Ravi had searched through the first batch of people who had gone missing. He had marked out about ten people that he felt he might have know from various points in his life. Most of these were people whose names and locations he felt vaguely familiar with, but he couldn't be sure. For example, he thought he knew a Nick Francis at school. He stuck in Ravi's mind as he had won some sort of TV art competition to design a stamp or something, and the school had made a bid deal of it. There was a Nick Francis on the list and his occupation had been stated as 'graphic designer'. That would make sense, thought Ravi.

Then there were a few people he thought he'd been to university with, one of his university professors and a woman that he sometimes chatted to who worked on the checkout at the local Tesco. There were also over a dozen names that seemed to match people from the social media links that he had cultivated. Altogether there were about twenty names.

Now what did he do...just wait and see if any of them showed up in pictures or videos? Was this really just an exercise to find out if he really was the catalyst for the Shaz? I suppose confirmation is useful, he thought to himself; if it really is people that I'm connected to that are at risk, I suppose we could warn anyone who has ever met me to get police protection, till we can work out what the hell's happening.

"Mr Popular or what!" he said out loud to himself, ironically.

To be honest, things had gone a little quiet since the sighting of the Shaz near the car: Ellie seemed to be spending more time talking to Matt and Elspeth in the lab, and Bruce seemed to be locked away in his study. Sometimes, Ravi thought that he could hear him talking to someone that sounded American on the video-link but then again it could have been a bad line.

Ravi started to think that they were all wasting their time. Perhaps it was even a big joke, like one of those Jackass stunts, where people dress up and leap out at unsuspecting victims to make them look like idiots. Perhaps the 'Shaz' were a big hoax and Bruce and Elspeth were eccentric old Scots, having a laugh at his expense? He'd settled into this line of thinking, when the next videos arrived.

"Quick, get in the study," Matt burst into the room to tell Ravi, "They've got some more people."

"What?" said Ravi, so wrapped up in his new theory that he almost didn't believe what Matt was saying.

"Get into the study, dude...The Shaz are sending some more stuff. It's like, getting worse man!"

Everyone gathered on the leather sofa and mismatched armchairs, facing the large, wall-mounted screen on the wall. Elspeth had noticed it flicker to life a few minutes earlier. On the screen had appeared a Shaz looking directly out of the screen and straight at her. This was no message sent by email; this was a live broadcast.

"We are here," the Shaz said; a female Shaz sidled in from the edge of the screen to be in the frame with her male compatriot.

We can see that, thought Ravi and the others, waiting anxiously on every word.

"We want to thank you for our new friends," she said gesturing into the distance.

"Holy shit," said Ravi and Matt together.

The camera panned across what looked like a community hall.

In the hall a group was gathered in two rows, one behind the other. In front was a group of Shaz, both male and female, a gap between each one. Directly behind each Shaz was a person. Ravi recognised Victoria Romerez and the others from the last pictures, he also recognised Nick Francis—older but definitely the same Nick that had gone to his school, and Professor Kunst from his university. Ravi thought he recognised another woman, blonde-haired and wearing a suit, but he couldn't put his finger on where he knew her from, or her name.

There were about twenty five people in the line and Ravi could point out about six of them, but he feared that he must also be linked to the others in some way. The fact that this must have been in a way that was relatively obscure, considering the fact that he did not recognise them, was very worrying.

"Who are the people you have gathered there," asked Bruce, the only one of them who seemed to be able to talk at all. "Why are you keeping them against their will?"

"They like it here. Don't you?" said the Shaz, nodding towards the group. Everyone in the lines, both Shaz and human nodded. The look of fear on the faces of the people did not correspond with their nods.

"Look, what is this about?" asked Ravi, despairingly. "If it is about me then let those people go and I'll take their place."

The others looked at Ravi, a dismayed look on all of their faces. Ellie shook her head vigorously.

"It's OK," he said, looking round at his companions, "I know I said that I wouldn't say that, but perhaps I can work it out with them when I'm there."

"No, we do not want that," the Shaz said. Ellie breathed a sigh of relief. "We do not need you here at present. We will be in contact with you. It is good to be learning from your people."

The Shaz started to turn around, preparing to leave.

"No, wait," said Ravi, "This is not fair! You can't just keep taking people like this."

"There is nothing that says it is not fair, Ravi," said the Shaz. "You know that. Goodbye."

The screen flickered off. Ellie had been furiously scribbling down what they had said.

"Look," said Bruce, "There is no point being shocked by this anymore. They clearly are not soft little loveable bunnies. We might need to get other people involved to stop this before it gets out of hand."

"Other people?" asked Ravi.

"Yes, the Special Extra-Terrestrial Unit that the big boys run: the SETU—co-funded by the US, India, China, Russia and Europe. I've been talking to my contact over in the States, I haven't told them too much, but maybe the time is right to get them involved."

"We talked about that though, " said Ellie, "We thought it was too risky...Those people could be killed."

"There might be a hell of a lot more people as good as dead, before too long by the looks of things," retorted Bruce, "The number of people they've taken seems to have increased quite a bit, don't you think? Yesterday two people, today twenty, tomorrow two hundred—get it?"

"But they all have to be connected to Ravi in some way don't they?" asked Ellie.

"Yeah well, how many of those people did you know personally, Ravi?" Bruce said, looking Ravi straight in the eye, "Don't you see that those things could connect anyone on earth to Ravi if they wanted to? Whilst we're sitting here deliberating they could be taking other people."

"You may be right about that," Ravi conceded, "But before we bring in the big guns, possible literally by the sounds of things, I suggest that we give it one last try to see whether we can work out what they want. We don't want to risk all-out war for the sake of a few days."

"Good point, dude," said Matt, encouragingly, "I don't want to be the cause of some sort of intergalactic war. Those little creatures could have some pretty big cousins, for all we know."

"None of us do, kid," said Bruce, "But the alternative could be worse."

"We don't know that, Bruce. I say it's too early to bring in the troops yet. I've just got a gut feeling about this," said Ravi. "Look, we've sent those tissue samples off to the outside labs right?...Well, what if we find out something about the Shaz that would help us overcome them? If we call your friends in now they might not want to wait for that."

"That's a good point," agreed Elspeth, "I think this is also about what the Shaz *are*, I feel that we could work something out about what makes them tick. I know that the government agencies have all of these experts, but we were the people that they came to all those years ago. There must be some reason for that."

"Look, why don't we do this," said Ravi, thinking of a possible compromise, "Is there someone you could trust to bring their team to work with us, in a low key style not reporting to anyone in the hierarchy?...Just fill them in on everything that's gone on without them taking over? That way if we find a way to sort this we can; if it looks like this is not going to be on the cards we can ask whoever it is to call in the reinforcements."

"Sounds like a good plan," agreed Ellie, "There must be someone, Bruce..."

Bruce still thought that this was potentially just delaying the inevitable, but he said that, if that was the consensus position, he'd agree to this compromise. Actually, though he didn't say anything to the others, he thought it was quite a good compromise. He'd try to figure out who to trust at SETU.

"Apart from the obvious fact that those people were scared shitless, did anyone notice anything about the broadcast," said Ellie, conscious of the fact that they were not able to replay it.

"They called people their 'friends'," said Elspeth, "This seems to tally with other comments that they've made."

" I thought I knew the woman in the red suit, that's about it really, sorry," said Ravi, "Oh, there was one other thing—what was that bit about learning?"

Ellie looked back at her notes. "The Shaz guy said near the end of the broadcast something about 'learning from us'."

"God, that sounds well creepy," said Matt, "Maybe it's, like, they're gonna take over our bodies."

"Or maybe they really do want to understand us and we have misjudged things?" suggested Elspeth.

"Whatever the explanation, we know that 'learning' is something that they are doing...might give us something to go on if we ever get to talk to them properly?" said Ravi.

"Listen," Elspeth said, her eyes wandering around at the weary-looking group, "We're all too tired to think of the next steps for tonight. Bruce, you'll get onto this person you know tomorrow?" Bruce nodded. "Ravi, you and Ellie might think about going down to London to talk to some of the friends and families of the people we saw on the screen there—they might be some help with understanding just how they went missing."

"Great idea," Ravi said enthusiastically, grateful that Elspeth, being the wise person that she was, had been quickly considering an immediate plan of action.

"And we," she said, nodding towards Matt, "We'll get on to those labs again and see if we can get anywhere with that finger. I think it may be time to take some new samples and take a closer look at it."

The scene was set then and the group melted away to different parts of the house.

Ravi continued to sit on the big leather sofa in the study, trying to work out what on earth he could say to someone whose son or daughter, close friend or sibling had suddenly disappeared. Would anyone even want to talk to him? he thought to himself. He concluded that, yes, they probably could be convinced to...after all, if someone you're close to goes missing, you'd clutch at any straws to help you try to get them back. Saying anything about the Shaz was a real no-no, of course; he could picture himself being thrown onto the street accused of being a total nut-case, hellbent on going around harassing vulnerable family members. No, it was definitely best to keep things low key. At least one thing worked in his favour: all of the people he was trying to find out about *knew* him, so hopefully this would open doors, albeit only a tiny bit. Still, it gave him something positive to work from.

There was one thing that was really worrying him. Doob was missing from the line-up of people with the Shaz.

BACK ON THE ROAD

Ravi and Ellie arrived back at the flat in Holly Road in the early evening and quickly set up a sort of mini control desk in the living area: print outs of all the key messages, names and photos of the abducted people, and the details of their initial contacts—the people that they wanted to talk to. They worked as a team, hardly saying anything until they were satisfied that everything was in order and that nothing had been missed out. Ravi thought back to the days when he, Doob and Matt dossed about on the sofa, playing X-box 360 and watching music videos, it seemed like a different world.

Ellie hooked up a laptop to the TV screen and browsed around to see if anything of interest was coming from any of their sources. It all seemed pretty quiet. They then looked around at news stories from the world's press to see if anything 'big' was hitting the wires: thankfully there was nothing. There was a story on the Bonnybridge Herald website about 'contact' made with aliens by local Professor Bruce McLeish, but Ellie said that this was not likely to be taken too seriously in the absence of any other information; Frank was well known for his enthusiasm on the topic.

They tuned the TV in to watch some 'normal' stuff—at the insistence of Ellie who said that Ravi was looking extremely tired and needed to chill out. They mindlessly watched a programme about bird life in the north-east of England and were sitting through an expose of people cheating the housing benefits system in London.

"Look, I think I'm going to bed now," yawned Ravi, "This isn't really my kind of thing."

"Mine neither," confessed Ellie, "Do you want to play a few games?"

By games Ravi knew that she meant on the Playstation and, yes, this was much more what he had in mind when he thought of relaxing. He was just about to switch over inputs to the screen when something caught his eye. The documentary droned on with some woman with a microphone—an investigative journalist, walking quickly alongside a swarthy looking man, who was trying to shield his face from the camera with a scarf. She was asking him about whether he owned five properties in West London and why, if this was the case, he was claiming housing benefit in three different names. It was not the man that had caught Ravi's attention, however, it was the woman. She was dressed differently, but it was the same blond-haired woman that he had half recognised amongst the other captives of the Shaz.

"That's the same woman," he said pointing at the screen, "The one that I thought I knew from the video." He re-wound the scene and paused at a frame where she looked around straight into the camera.

"The one in the suit?" Ellie said, squinting at the frozen image, "yes, I see what you mean...it could be the same person."

"It's her," said Ravi emphatically, "I thought I'd seen her somewhere; she's on a couple of things on the telly: one's this investigative thing and the other's a kind of talking about consumer affairs type programme.

"But she was just on the TV," said Ellie, "she looked fine."

Ravi looked at Ellie. She really could miss the obvious sometimes, for someone who had so many qualifications, he thought to himself. "Ellie, that was not a live broadcast; it was probably recorded months ago—it could have been a repeat from years ago." He fast forwarded to the closing credits, they listed the production as last year.

"Her name is Kirsty Wade, if she's gone missing that's bound to have created a bit more fuss that the average London Joe; people would link it to her work. We need to see if there are any local pieces on the news about her..."

They searched through the local TV news sites and local press. Nothing showed up. They *did* find some articles on Ravi's old lecturer: Professor Kunst and a lot on Sarah Wooley, including a very emotional plea from her parents for her to come home, saying that they were sorry if there was anything troubling her that they hadn't noticed, but they were there for her and just wanted her home. Ellie's eyes filled up watching the appeal, the Wooley's looked so racked with guilt and despairing. She offered to go with Ravi to see his old school-friend, Mark, Sarah's brother, if he wanted her to.

Ravi felt that it would only be a matter of time before things kicked off in terms of Kirsty Wade's disappearance, so, to pre-empt the media interest, he decided to call the production company that she worked for the next day on some pretext and try and find out what her movements had been just before she went missing. Then he realised something deeply troubling:

"Ellie," he said quietly, "This is bad...this is *really* bad."

Ellie looked back at Ravi, wondering what he meant and bracing herself for his next comment. "What do you mean?" she asked.

"What connection do I have with Kirsty Wade?" he asked. Ellie shrugged her shoulders.

"I'll tell you what connection I have, Ellie. Absolutely non! The only time I've seen her has been when I've watched her on TV," Ravi paused, "Think of the number of people I might have seen on TV, or online somewhere."

Their worst fears were being confirmed. If Kirsty Wade was taken just because Ravi had seen her on TV, where would it end?

"Ellie, I think that the Shaz are changing the rules of the game. They started with someone I knew well—a close friend. From there they took people I'd known from school, college and so on, Victoria Romerez doesn't quite fit—but, if they were using internet connections she could have been mistaken for someone closer to me: where people are located isn't that clear when you're going by internet connections. Then they moved on to people with whom I had no real connection with, past being in the same place sometimes—people that came into the shop, the woman who served me in the supermarket, that sort of thing."

Ellie could see what this was leading to. "So you mean that *anyone*..."

"Exactly," said Ravi, pre-empting what she was going to say, "They have moved on to people I have never met before. I'm effectively out of the picture and they are now taking anyone. If they *are* operating on the basis that the person should be connected to me in some way, I am sure that they can justify it to themselves with some vague link. Pretty soon though I get the feeling that they will just be taking people at random."

Ellie didn't want to say too much but it almost felt like they were at that stage already to her.

"Look, we need to get this info' to Bruce...he might be making some progress. Lets give, him a call," Ravi said, pulling out his phone. Instead of calling Bruce though, something made Ravi instinctively call the same number he had been trying to get hold of: the pay-as-you-go number that he had got the missed calls from on the day that he and Ellie had driven towards Bonnybridge and encountered the Shaz. He pressed the call button and held the phone to his ear. This time the phone did not go onto voicemail...

"Hello," a female voice sounded clearly on the other end of the phone, "Who is this?"

"This is Ravi...I've had some missed calls from your number."

"Oh God, Ravi! It's Angel here. I've just found this phone today and got it charged up... I had no idea." She was making no sense at all and sounded incredibly tense, firing out her words in between what sounded like sobs.

"Angel, take a deep breath, I can't make out what you're saying," said Ravi helplessly, "if you didn't call me from the phone who did?"

"Sorry Ravi," said Angel, trying audibly to compose herself, "I'm sorry, what I'm trying to tell you is that the phone was on Doob when I found him. Doob came here, to me!"

Ravi felt a surge of excitement and relief. At last there was some good news: a breakthrough. His friend was back.

"That is fantastic," Ravi was almost lost for words, "Put him on, let me speak to him then!"

"Ravi, no, its not like that. Doob arrived at my door a few days ago, but he was in a terrible state. He could hardly speak; just kept saying not to tell anyone he was back in case some people came and got him again...then he fell kind of into a daze. I called 999 straight away, I was so frighted. The paramedics took him to the Royal London but they don't know what's wrong with him. I think they've done loads of tests. He's been lying in a hospital bed since then, hardly conscious. I've been over there everyday. He does say things, but I can't make out a word of what he's saying." Angel spilled out the news, one point after another, hardly pausing for breath. She was clearly not coping very well and extremely worried about Doob. She told Ravi that she was just about to go back to the hospital with some of Doob's things (including an iPod and some music; the doctor had told her that patients sometimes recovered more quickly with auditory stimuli).

"Just wait for a while Angel, we'll come with you" said Ravi, I'm coming straight over.

Ravi and Ellie arrived at Angel's small apartment, above a dry cleaning shop in Haringey, about an hour later. Ravi was rather reluctant for Ellie to come at first, partly because he hadn't said anything to Angel about her and partly because he didn't know what sort of a state Doob would be in. From what Angel had said he sounded pretty delirious: apparently he didn't really know who Angel was, although he must have had *some* recollection, since he made it to her door (unless someone else had taken him there, of course?)

Angel opened the door, took one glance at Ravi and fell against him, sobbing, the metallic waves of her hair bobbing up and down as she cried. Ravi felt slightly uncomfortable and stood rather awkwardly until she had composed herself a little.

"Oh, Ravi, thank God you're here. Come in, come in." She spotted Ellie and looked at her quizzically, "Is she your girlfriend?" she asked.

"This is Ellie; she's moved into the flat," Ravi had to remind himself why Ellie had become part of his life in London.

Angel looked at Ellie in an accusatory way, as if she might have had a hand in what had happened to Doob, just to get hold of his room. Then she realised that this was nonsense: the girl had probably volunteered to come along with Ravi and was wondering what the hell was going on.

"It's OK..." continued Ravi, "Ellie knows about Doob. She's been a big help. You can trust her."

Ellie was a little taken about. *She* can trust *me*?...she questioned, then she realised that she was being more than a little sensitive, given the situation, after all Ravi had known Angel for a lot longer than he had known her, let alone the fact that she had never even met Doob. Your Scottish pride is getting to you, she thought to herself guilty.

"Hello," Ellie outstretched her hand towards the still quivering Angel. Angel took the hand in both of hers and gestured them both inside.

Angel recounted the story more fully to Ravi, not that there was a lot more to add. He had arrived, as she had said and collapsed at the door. The paramedics had arrived within ten minutes and had seemed extremely worried about Doob, taking him straight to hospital. He bypassed all of the emergency room procedures and was rushed straight in to see one of the consultants, who had him admitted immediately to Intensive Care as he had extremely erratic vital signs. Since then, Doob had had a series of tests to ascertain what was wrong with him but, though the neurotransmitters in his brain seemed to be acting very strangely, he had not had some sort of stroke (which they had first suspected). They were still searching the answer to whatever was wrong with Doob.

Angel had seen some glimmerings of hope. Initially, Doob had been in some sort of delirium, thrashing about uncontrollably and hitting out against an unseen enemy, occasionally weeping hysterically and pleading for help. The doctors had given him a sedative, which basically knocked him out and, as it was wearing off, Doob seemed to be regaining some of his mind. He had looked at Angel with recognition and she had even him smile. He had also tried to say a few words to her, looking urgently into her eyes, indicating the importance of what it was he was trying to say, but she couldn't make out the words yet. Angel warned Ravi and Ellie not to expect too much for now.

As they went through the door to the intensive care room, Ravi was praying hard to any God that would listen to help his friend recover.

Doob was lying in bed, apparently asleep. His skin had a sort of waxy look to it and he was breathing heavily, as if it was a great strain. A few tubes were connected to Doob, possibly to help to administer medication or fluids (Angel said that they were also monitoring things about this brain function), but he was no longer on the ventilator that he had been on when he had first been admitted. Although Ravi had watched quite a few hospital dramas, he felt overwhelmed by the sight of his friend lying helpless in that small room. Ellie was pretty stoic—having been brought up by a doctor she was pretty familiar with the realities of hospitals and modern medicine.

Every now and then Doob cried out unintelligibly. Ravi was used to seeing Doob sauntering about the place with his usual swagger, seeing his gleaming smile and hearing his wicked one-liners captivating anyone that met him. Doob was always the one in the room that was in control; the person that others looked to for a steer. For Ravi the contrast with the clay like shape lying in the bed before him was heartbreaking. Then he realised that this *was* Doob: he was alive and he was here, in front of him! He had managed to get away from the Shaz and make it back to safety. It was the breakthrough they had been looking desperately for, thought Ravi, suddenly feeling optimistic. Doob was going to get better, although life would never be the same again, for either of them.

Ravi sat on the edge and reached over to put his hand on Doob's shoulder.

"It's me, bro—Ravi," he said quietly, "I've missed you man."

There was no movement, or hint of recognition from Doob, his breathing continued in the same heaving way.

"Look Doob, 'you the man', you've got to get through this, all right?" No reaction, "All right Doob...?"

"Ravi, we need to be patient, we don't know how much trauma he's been through," Ellie butted in, gently. She got some chairs; it was going to be a long hour.

Angel had said that Doob had started to recognise her and that he had tried to say something to her, something important. However, now it seemed like Doob was lost in a world of his own and wasn't reacting to anything again; Ravi felt disappointed, cheated even: he had believed that if Doob was going to want to speak to anyone it would be him. Then it dawned on him that Doob was very sick and that maybe his expectations were rather too high. In his head, Ravi's emotions were all over the place.

He thought that Doob was gesturing towards him, but Angel said that he did that sometimes, as if re-living something that he had experienced. Angel tried playing some of the soulful music she had brought, but he groaned and thrashed about when he heard it, so she turned it off. Doob's reaction to the music they knew that he loved did not correlate: Doob *always* had tunes on his 'phones or playing in the background. Something had really messed up his head.

"Let's head back, Ravi" said Ellie eventually, "Nothing's going to happen tonight. We can come back tomorrow if you like, and Angel will keep us updated." Angel nodded.

Ravi got up to leave and just at that moment heard Doob whisper his name, quietly but definitely. Ravi sat back down looking intently at Doob. Slowly, Doob started to talk—in a slow laboured way, but what he was saying was unmistakable. He had opened his eyes and looked at Ravi and pleaded with him.

"Ravi. Stop them. The game...teach... music...."

Then he looked around for Angel:

"Tired," he said to her, "Angel." He closed his eyes and fell silent.

Ravi looked down at the floor, fearing that he had died. He felt a hand on his shoulder and looked around to see Eliie.

"I don't know what you're crying for Rav," she said, "Your friend has done really well, he's just resting after all that exertion."

Ellie had not been brought up by an eminent doctor for nothing.

MORE MISCHIEF

The next day Ravi seemed to have found some renewed energy. The return of Doob gave the whole team a boost and there were lots of questions from Edinburgh about his condition. Elspeth said that it sounded as if Doob was suffering from some sort of post-traumatic shock, and that she could come down and try to help if they liked. She told them that, if it was PTSD, this would take a long time (years, decades even) for him to recover and that this period was critical; they needed to be very careful not to expect too much too soon.

When Ravi next spoke to Angel he passed on Elspeth's advice, although he knew that she was speaking more to him than to anyone else. Angel said that actually Doob was doing 'a lot better' as she put it and had said a few words to her. He had even managed to eat something and was resting again. She sounded very, very relieved. Ravi asked Angel to keep updating him and said that he would get over there to see them again later that day.

The team tried to work out what Doob could have meant in his laboured message to Ravi. Were he and the others involved in some strange game? What was the relevance of music and teaching? Was Doob released or did he escape? Until Doob could tell them more there were many unanswered questions. The consensus was, however, that the kidnapped people were in critical danger. The Shaz were not friendly harmless allies.

The plan was still to contact people that knew those that they had seen with the Shaz—but now they didn't rule out more of them turning up: traumatised but alive. It was better than not turning up at all.

Ravi and Ellie started to try to find out what was happening to the others they had seen. Over cups of coffee they continued to scan the media for reports of people going missing or even being found, keeping the hotline open to Edinburgh for updates.

Bruce had sent them a new list of possible abductees, but Ravi had ignored it, feeling that since there were so many it was better to concentrate on the people they already knew about—especially Doob, rather than just keep adding to the list. Out of the previous missing people no-one else had been found. Media attention on the missing schoolgirl—Sarah Wooley was still prominent and had hit the national news headlines.

It was not just Sarah who had made the news. Ravi noticed a piece on Kirsty Wade in the local bulletin. Kirsty had been reported missing by her boyfriend, who felt that she may have been kidnapped (or worse) because of a story she was doing about some political group in the Caucasus region. It was not her usual kind of thing, he said, but she had wanted to move into a higher bracket in terms of investigative journalism—and that meant entering dangerous journalistic territory. The poor boyfriend looked distraught, also a journalist (with a national newspaper) he understood the danger she was in, he said. Ravi took a note of his name, Ben Rogers and decided that he'd try to get to see him: he looked desperate to find out what had happened to Kirsty and Ravi thought that he would agree to give him further details, if he could convince him that he could help (this was going to be tricky but he thought that Ellie might help with this). He sent Ben an email; he must have been online at the time because Ravi got a message back straight away agreeing to meet.

An hour and a half later Ravi and Ellie had arrived in the hotel lobby in West London where Ben had agreed to meet them. He looked like he hadn't slept for a while. He grabbed their hands energetically to greet them and thanked them for coming:

"I know something's wrong," he said, "Kirsty would never just disappear like that. The studio is just not taking it seriously at all. Infact, I get the feeling that they think we must have had some sort of row and that's she's gone off in a huff...I know she's strong willed, but that's just rubbish. She is a very responsible person."

Ravi had already told Ben that what he had to say was pretty bizarre, but Ben had said that any clues as to her whereabouts, no matter how odd it sounded, would be of help. So Ravi decided to take the plunge:

"Look, Ben...this is going to sound very, very barmy," he paused and took a deep breath, "A friend of mine went missing too a number of months ago and we received strange messages about him, together with photos. That friend has now got back to us, he's recovering from his ordeal and we're waiting to find out more about what happened to him."

"Photos?" said Ben, "I haven't heard anything. Were they like those pictures you sometimes see on the news with political messages behind? Was it a terrorist group?"

"No...not exactly," continued Ravi, nervously. "Our friend was abducted by people who made him participate in some sort of activity, we don't know exactly what yet. But, he was taken against his will and we think your girlfriend was taken in the same way."

"OK, OK...You say you've got pictures. Have you got any pictures of the people who kidnapped your friend—I mean were they wearing masks or anything? Were they speaking with any sort of accent?"

"They weren't exactly wearing masks, no," said Ellie slowly, "In fact, they weren't exactly people."

"What do you mean, they were inhuman brutes?" Ben paled, "The activity you're talking about...it wasn't *sexual* was it?" He really feared the worst.

"No, no, nothing like that, as far as we know."

Ellie and Ravi looked at each other as if trying to decide whether they could go on. Ravi nodded. Ellie took out her tablet and browsed through on the screen until she found what she was looking for: a slideshow of the photos and messages that had been sent by the Shaz.

"We think that these things have got Kirsty captive; we've already identified some other people that are in the same predicament," she passed over the computer to Ben for him to see. "Look, we know it seems far-fetched but I've seen things and so has Ravi. I know you might think this is insane but we are normal people and this is getting serious."

Ben looked at the screen, his face contorting slightly.

"Are you serious?" said Ben, his voice quivering with distress, "Is this some sort of sick joke?"

Ellie and Ravi looked at one another once again, feeling that perhaps they had made the wrong decision.

"I'm sorry, but my girlfriend is missing, she could be locked up somewhere in the hands of terrorists, she could even be dead and you ask to meet to show me—THIS." Ben threw the tablet back at Ellie and stood up. "I'm sorry you've wasted your time," he said, clearly furious, "Please take your little fantasy elsewhere."

"Don't go," said Ellie frantically, "Please let us explain."

"Let it go, Ellie," said Ravi, trying to stay calm, "Let him go."

"We'll send you the names of some of the people, so you can check...It's NOT a joke!" said Ellie, calling after Ben, who was storming towards the hotel exit.

"Goodbye," he waved across his shoulder sarcastically as he disappeared out of view.

"Well, that went well," said Ravi, conscious that the hotel staff were looking at them, "I think we better leave."

They walked to the tube station looking sullen.

"People won't believe us until something awful happens," said Ellie quietly.

"Nothing awful is going to happen, " said Ravi, hoping to reassure her, "Look, Doob's back isn't he?" Inside he had an awful feeling that Doob had been incredibly lucky compared to what could have happened—what could happen to the others.

"Yes...I guess so," said Ellie but really she was very unconvinced. She had seen the state that Doob was in and realised that, even if Doob had been freed by the Shaz rather than escaping, it must have been touch and go for him to survive for a few days, and he was a fit adult man in his twenties; what about people older, younger or more frail than him?

"Let's go and see Doob right, now, " Ravi suggested, "Angel said he was looking stronger. He might be able to fill in some of the gaps for us."

"OK," agreed Ellie, let's go.

By the time they reached the Royal London Hospital it was dark. The building was a hive of activity, as always, but the ward itself had dimmed lighting, which gave it a somewhat warm and inviting feel. Angel had been sitting next to Doob's bedside pretty much all day, on and off; watching for the brief periods when he had opened his eyes and looked at her. Spotting Ellie and Ravi looking through the window of the door, she came out to talk to them without disturbing Doob. She was not sure just how much he could hear or understand, but the doctors had said that he would probably be able to hear everything some time before he could actually respond, so she didn't want him to hear anything that might alarm him and put back his recovery.

"He's a lot better," said Angel encouragingly, "You might not notice the difference, cos he's still not saying much...but I can tell.

He has even been able to say a couple of words—asking for water, stuff like that, but it's not all the time. Most of the time he's still really out of it."

Ravi sat quietly next to Doob. He definitely looked better, he seemed to have more elasticity in his face and his skin seemed less waxy. He just looked as if he was having a bit of a rest, his chest rising slowly up and down with a gentle and consistent rhythm. The nurses had told them that they could spend half an hour with Doob, to avoid undue stress, so they did not have much time.

"Hey, Doob. It's me again, Ravi," he said gently, "How are you bro?"

Doob moved his hand slightly. All three of them watched carefully as he turned the hand to rest on it's side and then, very slowly lifted his thumb. He was giving them a thumbs up.

"Doob, can you talk?" continued Ravi, "We want to know what happened to you...oh and before I forget, this is Ellie, she is here to help: to help stop this happening to anyone else."

"Will try," said Doob, his voice croaking and weak.

"Thanks, Doob," said Ellie, "Hey, what if we just ask you some questions and you just say yes or no to start with? Then if you feel stronger you can tell us all about it in your own words." Ellie had remembered the old 'twenty questions' game and thought that this would save on Doob's energy. Doob once again gave them the thumbs up.

"Doob we've received some images, but we don't want to show them to you in case it upsets you. So we'll just talk to you instead for now," Ellie spoke in a quiet and reassuring voice. Doob slightly nodded his head.

"Do you remember being taken?" Again an affirmative answer.

"Were you held against your will?" Doob gave her a thumbs up.

"This is going to sound a bit weird, but were you taken by human beings?" Doob's hand lay flat against the bed, he shook his head.

"Were you taken by...I can't think of a better way to describe them...*aliens*?" Doob nodded.

Ellie looked around at Ravi. "You're doing really well, " he said squeezing her hand.

"Hey, bro. We know about those things. We are going to stop this," he said calmly to Doob, "Just stick with us, Doob."

Ellie continued, keeping the same steady pace and gentle demeanour. "We need to know Doob, did they harm you?" Doob indicated yes. They could see that he was trying to say something. Angel came closer and held his hand.

"How did they hurt you, baby?" she said, drawing close to him. "What did they do?"

Doob looked at Angel and forced out the word 'head'. They had done something to his mind.

OK...this confirmed everything that they already suspected, thought Ravi, but how were they going to stop people being taken...and free those that were already captive.

"Doob, did the aliens let you go?" There was no response.

"He doesn't know," said Ellie, "Perhaps he can't remember; it is pretty common when the mind has been damaged by stuff."

"OK," Ravi continued, "We need to know how they managed to abduct you. Can you remember that?" Doob nodded. "Please try to tell us," asked Ravi, he knew that this would involve more than a yes or no; he just hoped that Doob was strong enough to respond.

Doob looked down slightly at the bed on which he was lying. The others followed his gaze over the white cotton honeycombed regulation hospital blanket and onto the brown laminate over-bed table On their arrival, Ravi and Ellie had absent mindedly put a few of their things on the table: mobiles, gloves, Ravi's 'man-bag' and so on, they'd pick the stuff up again when they left.

"He's looking for something," said Ellie, moving over to the table. Object by object she asked Doob what it was he wanted to show them. Doob remained impassive until Ellie held up her small tablet computer. Doob nodded.

"Something about the internet, did you get a message from someone...was that it Doob? Ravi was excited: it all seemed to fit. The messages from domino236ot, the photos, the videos—some way of entrapping people using the web would make perfect sense"

Doob nodded once again. He was once again trying to say something.

"What is it, Doob, what it is brother? What did the message say. Did it threaten you, blackmail you?"

Doob shook his head.

"Wait Ravi, Can't you see he's trying to say something? Just let him speak," said Angel, crossly.

"What is it babe? Just take your time," she said to Doob gently, putting her ear next to his mouth.

"Teach, travel." Doob closed his eyes, exhausted.

"That's just about enough now. You'll have to let your friend rest." The nurse, that had appeared at the door, reminded them that their agreed time was up.

"OK, that's fine, we'll just be saying our goodbyes," said Ravi. He waited for the nurse to close the door before he asked his final question.

"Doob, we need to know how many people have been taken. I'm sorry, bro, 'cos I know you're tired. Are you OK to answer just one more question?

Doob signalled that he would do this. Ravi continued.

"OK, dude we know there are about twenty people in the files that we've been sent. Are there more than that number, Doob?"

"Yeah," said Doob, weakly.

"How many more?" asked Ravi nervously, starting to feel a bit sick in anticipation of Doob's answer, "Fifty...sixty?"

Doob turned his head to look directly at Ravi ominously.

"Bro, hundreds...more" Doob turned his head back and closed his eyes.

"I'm sorry, you really have to leave," the nurse insisted, as she walked into the room, "There's too many of you. You have to leave. Thank you."

NEW REALITIES

The revelation that there were at least hundreds of people that had been taken was a multiple blow to the team: they were failing to detect more of the kidnappings, the abductions must now be fairly random and not linked to Ravi anymore, and the rate of abduction could possibly be increasing exponentially.

Ravi and Ellie postulated that the 'modus operandi' of the Shaz was to send some sort of message—possibly an email or a social media message, to the victim and try to lure the person into a trap. The message, in Doob's case anyway, could incorporate something about teaching and the potential of travel (could it be that the Shaz were using a basic technique of offering the recipient some opportunity or other...some lure that got the reader interested in, essentially, a scam?).

They faced a huge dilemma. How were they going to be able to gain the attention of anyone at all, when the reaction of Ben had shown that even people closely connected to victims didn't take them seriously? Despite the fact that, according to Doob, so many people had been taken, their disappearances seemed to have made no dent in the system and they had not been taken up by the media. When Ravi remembered the long lists of names given to him by Bruce, he could see how even a few hundred names could be lost amongst thousands. It would take something spectacular to grab people's attention—more than the few images that they possessed and that would be branded as fakes. The problem was that 'something spectacular' was likely to involve the capture of hundreds more, possibly thousands of people, affecting millions of lives: affecting the life of every single person on the planet.

Two things then happened that, in quick succession, meant that bringing the issues into the public spotlight was taken out of the hands of Ravi and Ellie.

Bruce and the others in Edinburgh had been desperately trying to get in touch with Ravi and Ellie but, because of the urgency of communicating with Doob, they had not been able to devote themselves to answering their messages for a day or so. When Ellie opened up her mail she gasped and understood even more the gravity of the situation.

They looked at the link sent by Bruce, reading it over and over, not wanting to believe their eyes. Mr Tranter, Ravi's old maths teacher had been found DEAD—*murdered*—in London along with an unknown woman, possibly a foreign national judging by the identification that she had on her. They suspected immediately that this was Victoria Romerez.

Their bodies had been found on wasteland near to the River Thames at the Isle of Dogs together with a message, the article said. The article did not elaborate on what the message said; Bruce had said in his mail that this was standard police practice as they did not want to give away vital information that might identify the perpetrators. Only the real perpetrators would know the contents of the message (in this way preventing the kind of false confessions that seemed to happen with these sorts of crimes). Since Mr Tranter was known to have been missing, the police were considering some sort of criminal gang involvement, but they were keeping an open mind. They were in touch with colleagues in Interpol about the other victim. The cause of their deaths was not revealed in the article.

Ellie quickly looked up the latest about the murders; there was not a great deal more out there, apart for the fact that there *was* increased concern expressed about some other missing people, including young Sarah Wooley. The Metropolitan Police had also found something that meant that they were looking again at some 'cold cases' that they had put on hold. Surely the Shaz had not been taking people for years? thought Ravi. Then he remembered the little Indian girl who, for him, was where it all started; that had been years ago, he remembered, perhaps this *had* been going on for a very long time.

Local papers had praised Mr Tranter as a 'community-minded and enthusiastic teacher', Ravi remembered him as being rather mediocre and not terribly good at communicating with his pupils. Infact, Ravi had always blamed Mr Tranter for his initial failure in GCSE maths (although he did get a 'B' when he re-took the exam a few months later). Despite his possible failings as a teacher, Ravi had no doubt that he was a good man.

The team got together by video-link to think what could be done. Bruce told Ravi and Ellie that he'd been in touch with SETU, but he couldn't reach the contact that he had hoped to involve. He was not sure now who to trust there; it was a bit of a wild card situation. The consensus from his other contacts seemed to be that involving SETU would lead to a dramatic escalation of the situation. As far as Ravi could see this was possibly becoming inevitable, now that people were dying.

Off the link, he and Ellie were of one mind: if no-one else was going to do anything, then they would. Even if the whole world thought that they were complete loons they would make the loudest noise possible. At the very least, the Shaz would get to know about it and would react in some way; they had to risk the people who had already been captured to prevent a potentially slow erosion of the human race.

Just as they were discussing their strategy a call came through on Ravi's phone. He did not recognise the number. His heart stopped, could it be them, could it be the Shaz?

"Hello," he said tentatively.

"Hello, Ravi, it's Ben here, you remember—Kirsty's partner.

Listen, I'm sorry about what happened last time we met, I hope you understand." Ben sounded even more distraught than the last time they had spoken.

Ravi said that it was no problem at all and asked if he had heard anything about Kirsty.

"Yes, yes I have. I don't know if you've seen on the news about the teacher guy, a Mr Tranter, I think you might have known him...I've heard about him too. I don't know where to start really. I think we need to meet."

"OK," said Ravi, gesturing to Ellie, "Where and when?"

Ben had invited Ravi and Ellie to his flat in Islington, which confirmed to Ravi that something had happened that meant that Ben now trusted them and needed their help. They were ushered into the swish, open plan lounge, furnished in white, with black leather Scandinavian designed seating. Ben looked worse for wear and Ravi wondered if he had been drinking.

"Look, you two, I'm just going to be upfront with you," started Ben, "When you showed me those pictures last time, of course I thought it was a load of crap. Aliens abducting people off the streets of London...it's the kind of thing you see on an old B movie, right?"

They agreed that it did seem far fetched.

"Well, there's been that story on the news over the past few days—the couple of people murdered by the river. Well, I recognised the name from the list that you gave me: a Mr Tranter." Ben paused and poured himself some water, offering a glass to Ravi and Ellie.

"You may have seen in the news, that it was reported that there were messages left on the bodies, but it was not disclosed what those messages were." Ben took a gulp of water. "Well, I know what the messages said, because information about them was delivered to me at my work email address, along with some other stuff. I want you to see what I was sent."

Ben dimmed the lights in the apartment and switched on the large monitor which virtually covered one of the smaller walls. As they watched, image after image came up, videos similar to the one that Doob had been in, only in these several people were in the frame with several Shaz. The videos showed people sitting in what appeared to be small labelled cubicles, each housing one person and a Shaz. They could not understand what the labels said. Both people and Shaz were wearing headphones and appeared to be quietly concentrating on something.

Ravi nudged Ellie, "That looks really creepy."

"Shh...urged Ben, this is the bit that..." his voice tailed off ominously.

On the screen, a couple of the Shaz went up to the person sitting in front of them—their 'teacher', if you will. The man had his head bowed, as if listening intently to whatever was playing on the headphones. The Shaz nudged the man and he fell down, off his chair and onto the floor. The image panned in to the fallen man. It really was a teacher: it was Mr Tranter; he lay motionless on the floor, staring upwards.

"He's dead," said Ellie.

"I think so," said Ben, "And that's not all...watch."

The screen showed five more cubicles, all with the same scene played out. Then the horrifying scale of the operation was revealed as an aerial shot zoomed out, showing literally *hundreds* of small, cell-like cubes, each with their own 'teacher' and 'pupil'.

Finally, there was a gruesome display of the corpses of the dead humans; all lined up and with the word 'reject' pinned to their clothing. Mr Tranter and Victoria Romerez were amongst them. A Shaz filled the screen and made a statement.

"Ravi, these people are not effective. We are returning them and will need to get replacements." The Shaz sounded naïve and regretful, as the others had in the past. The video ended.

Ben rewound part of it and zoomed in, stopping at a frame. It was the ariel shot, high above the 'hive' but he had zoomed in to one particular 'cell'.

"As soon as I saw it, even from a distance I knew it was her," he said, his voice straining under the pressure, "I knew it was Kirsty."

The image was unmistakably that of his girlfriend, sitting just like the others, wearing a pair of headphones.

"At least she's not dead yet," he said gloomily.

"Who else has seen the tape?" asked Ellie, "We need to do something, quickly."

"No-one, as far as I know, but they might have sent them to other outlets...the TV...the news wires. It could have gone round the globe. What *can* we do?"

"We have to warn people without causing mass hysteria. I don't think it's going to be particularly easy. We have to buy a bit of time, so that we can work out a way to persuade them or destroy them and get those people, including Kirsty, out alive, " said Ravi. "We think that whatever they are, they are trying to *learn* from us, without realising that we can't deliver the goods. Goodness knows how many people are going to be sacrificed before they work that one out!"

"Please, just think of a way to get Kirsty out of there," pleaded Ben, "She's everything I've got."

"What time does your paper go to print?" asked Ravi, "The print and the online edition."

"It varies...about four am for the first editions; online, we can change during the day, if something big comes in."

"...and you can spread a message round the wires pretty easily?"

"You can't stop it, once its out there it spreads like wildfire: globally... but, hang on a minute, I'm not the editor; I'd never be able to get a story up without the editor's say so. Everything is completely locked down."

"What's your editor like?"

"He's OK. I don't really meet him that much but he seems like a decent kinda guy; interested in a knighthood, like all of them."

"Call him: we're running out of options. We're just gonna have to open this up and hope that the big guys act like professionals. Ellie, you call Bruce straight away, see if he's got anything out of this SETU place that can help us. "

"Things look as if they might already be moving," said Ben, looking at his phone, "I've just got a message from my boss asking to see me."

"Call him," said Ravi, taking control, "If it's not about the situation with these things—we call them the Shaz—then tell him about them and what's happening and make sure he agrees to see us about it, tonight."

Ben called the editor back, it *was* about the Shaz. Tony Ferrante, editor of the UK Tribune had seen the video, not because a link was sent directly to him, but from a Frank Tobin who worked for some local rag in Scotland. The guy wanted big money for it and was threatening to print it himself. This guy Frank had also spotted someone that he thought was Kirsty Wade and was sure that this made the video very valuable, he'd said.

"Look, Ben, I don't want you to be upset by all this...The guy and the video are obviously part of some insane, messed up, sick fantasist stuff; the thing is though," Tony paused, "The people on that video, the dead ones, they do look real. If this is the start of something big, we should be on it first. We might need to strike a deal with this Tobin man."

Ben had told Tony that he might not have to: he had been sent the same video.

"In that case, Ben," said the seasoned, wily editor, "Come along to my office tomorrow and we'll see what to run with. We're going to have to take a risk with this one, but I've got a gut feeling about it. Oh, and I'm sorry about Kirsty, I hope it's not her in the film...my guess is that the dead guys are real enough and the rest of it is staged as part of some weird, mentally screwed-up shit. I've seen it before: there was that hoax staging of a shark attack we got thirty years ago, turned out to be drugs bandits in Colombia feeding their rivals to some of the local wildlife."

Ben suggested that they meet that night; he had some people that he wanted Tony Ferrante to meet—people who could throw some more light on the whole story. Tony insisted that tomorrow would be fine; he had a keen sense of what was urgent and what could wait till the next day, he said and this could wait till the morning. He'd get some of his people to check the authenticity of the video and get back to him about it. If most of the video was a hoax, as he thought it was, then they'd contact the authorities after printing the exclusive. The ET man—Frank, was nothing to worry about now they had their own copy; he'd take care of speaking to him.

ADJUSTMENT

Ravi was in the headquarters of the UK Tribune with Ben (Ellie had gone over to see Doob in hospital to see whether he was improving and whether he could give them any more information about how he had been abducted). The building, near Clerkenwell, was a multi-storied hive of efficiency, though most of it seemed to be given over to anonymous business services, rather than reporting, as far as Ravi could tell. On the other hand Ravi had no idea what a floor full of reporters actually looked like. When he got to the floor that Ben worked on, he found out.

Small groups of work stations housed casual looking journalists, tapping into laptops or scrolling through stuff on-screen. Everyone seemed to be concentrating hard on the job in hand and the place had the feel of restless urgency, with people occasionally on their phones, foreheads contorted into looks of concern. There were always decisions to be taken, deals to be made and deadlines to be met, Ben informed Ravi.

Along the side of one wall was a series of meeting rooms, glass-walled, with a fancy system where the glass went from clear to opaque when someone flicked a switch. Tony's office was at the end of the row. He was already waiting for them, sitting at a large desk housing the minimum that he required: a photograph of his family, a couple of phones and an old-fashioned Rolodex of index cards of his closest allies and bitterest rivals. He liked to know what was going on with both sets of people. His prim looking secretary, Ms Woods, was seated at the board table, as was a thin man in his thirties, wearing a striped shirt and glasses (from image services, guessed Ben correctly—must be there about the authenticity of the video). Tony gestured for them to have a seat at the table with the other two. He obscured the view to the room and joined them.

"OK, Ben, first of all, tell me who your friend is and why he is here. We've got some decisions to make and I need to know that we can trust everyone sitting around this table," said Tony. He had the air of a rather well-off uncle, an air of authority and confidence borne of making the right decisions and being respected and feared for that. He looked Ravi straight in the eye; weighing up whether he was a problem or was going to be useful to him.

Ben explained that Ravi had brought him similar evidence to the video—but that he had ignored it, which he now regretted. He said that Ravi and a friend of his had direct contact with the situation and could possibly negotiate with whoever it was that was sending the images. It was Ravi, he said, that was going to provide them with the story.

Tony looked at Ravi with a degree of distrust, he was not that convinced, however, he decided that he would give Ben the benefit of the doubt; Ravi didn't *look* like a nut-case, or a spy from a rival paper, and they needed to move fast on the story.

"OK, kid...I'll tell you what we've got," Tony said, directing his comment at Ravi, "We've got a video that checks out in terms of the technicals but not in terms of some of the crackpot content. Part of it includes real people that have been murdered and a general threat that more people will be taken. The kidnappers appear to be part of some weird sci-fi role playing club. What have you got on it?" Tony looked at Ravi with a degree of amusement...this could get pretty freaky, he thought to himself.

Ravi relayed the story of how Doob had been taken by the same 'people'. He decided to leave off trying to convince Tony that the Shaz were not human: he had to tackle one thing at a time, and he had a plan to try to prevent a few people at least falling victim to the Shaz's scam messages. He said that Doob had basically fallen victim to a scam where he had been offered some sort of teaching opportunity, possibly to teach 'people' about some aspect of music production, DJing or the like. When he had answered the message he had somehow been lured away and captured. Ravi was not exactly sure that this was the exact story, but he was sure that it was pretty close to it. He didn't know whether this was the same way that everyone was 'recruited' but, in the absence of any other theory, it seemed reasonable to believe that the internet featured heavily in both the choice of victims and communication with them. Even Ravi had been identified by a username.

"OK, so what we've got is a group of psychos, dressed as aliens, who send out messages offering random people (Ravi had deliberately missed out the information that, at least the early victims, were connected to him in some way) the chance to travel and teach stuff that they know to other weird goon kids?" confirmed Tony.

"That's just about it in a nutshell," agreed Ravi, trying to rise above the fact that, laid out in basic terms, it did sound pretty weird—and the actual real story was even weirder.

"Right, well I've decided not to ignore it," said Tony, after a few minutes of contemplation, "Partly because there are elements that are clearly real and dangerous; we want to be in on breaking anything that smells like a breakthrough, or protects other people. We're going to have to turn the video over to the police—we don't want to piss off the boys in blue, or the public- but I'll try to keep you out of the spotlight young man," he said, nodding at Ravi. "OK, Ben you get a piece ready and I'll take a look at it. I'm thinking first edition tomorrow."

And that was it, the decision had been made. The world, or at least the UK, was going to see its first pictures of the Shaz. Ben worked on the article, making it not too alarming but urging people to be very cautious about responding to emails or social media messages about teaching or tutoring, especially if there was the promise that this would involve anything 'unusual' or seemed vague. He hoped that it would not be buried on page twenty three. As it happened he needn't have worried.

Ravi went back over to the hospital to see Doob after the visit to the newspaper headquarters. He was greeted by the amazing sight of Doob dressed in his normal clothes, though sitting in a wheelchair, Ellie and Angel beamed at Ravi as he came came through the swing doors to the room.

"Doob's coming home," said Angel ecstatically, bobbing up and down with excitement, "He shouldn't really: they want to keep him in for observation, but he's just made such an amazing, miracle recovery that the doctors have said that they can't stop him. He's still weak, but it's like whatever had a hold on him has left him. Ravi, I think he's going to be back to the old Doob again!"

Doob smiled up at Ravi, he looked like a completely different person.

"Hiya, Bro," said Ravi, relieved, "Man, you had us worried."

Despite appearances, Doob was not going to go home that day, he'd conceded that maybe he should be at the hospital for one more day to test out his amazing recovery, he had decided to go home the next day if things held up.

Ravi told everyone about the meeting at the UK Tribune HQ. He wondered how close he had got to the real story that Doob had been trying to let them know, only a day or so ago: It turned out that he was pretty close. Doob told them, slowly but steadily, that he had responded to an email, from an agency by the looks of things, offering him the chance to teach others about his 'passion' (in his case music) in the location of his dreams. Being Doob, he was intrigued by this and had replied to the message. He could not remember anything after that till his strange and frightening experience with the Shaz. He was sort of hooked up with a Shaz and, through some sort of headphone device, made to transfer his knowledge to it. Doob's head bowed as he recalled the agony of the information being prised from his mind.

Ellie asked him how the Shaz were with each other and with him, but he only recalled it as being a strange 'netherworld', where he could see many other people but couldn't communicate with them. He had tried to speak to a young girl he saw there, who he thought he vaguely recognised (could she have been Sarah Wooley? thought Ravi) but both of them felt excruciating pain as a result. He did not know how he had managed to get away, or how he had ended up at Angel's door. He also knew nothing about the Eastern European man or leaving the headphones for Ravi.

"Don't worry," said Ellie, "Perhaps you were just lucky: they just made a mistake and you ended up being sent back. The headphones seem to be associated with what you went through, but they could just be a red herring...anyway, it's immaterial now that things have moved on so much."

"Look," said Ravi anxiously, "Is there anything that you saw that could give us something to work on in terms of a weakness? Is there something that they want in order to leave us alone? Doob could not identify anything, he just knew that the Shaz were not thinking of winding down their activities anytime soon, by the looks of things.

"Thousands of rooms...when I was leaving. Like they were empty, dude, but they were there."

The next morning, Ravi went down to the newsagents on the corner of Holly Road to get a UK Tribune. The front page announced some story about how the banking crisis was set to re-emerge. Ravi, for whatever reason, thought that perhaps the Shaz story had not made it to the printers, perhaps Tony Ferrante had thought the better of it, after all? But, as he turned the page, there it was, facing him on page three:

"Murders linked to bizarre group operating email scam."

Exactly as they had discussed, the article suggested that the recent deaths may have been connected to people responding to messages about teaching opportunities. Ben had done a good job, he thought, maintaining the fine line between being over sensational and too downbeat. Back at the flat Ravi and Ellie went online to see what the reaction was.

So far, not that much, thought Ravi as they searched to see what the reaction from other sections of the press had been. They decided to check in with the others in Scotland and, when they did, realised how premature their assessment had been.

"Ellie, Ravi, do you remember that journalist, the one that I told you about Frank Tobin?"

"Yeah, the one that also had the video of the Shaz; he contacted Tony Ferrante offering to sell it but they already had their own copy. We were just going to call you about the article that Ben wrote, it's good but it doesn't make direct reference to *them*, so I'm not sure how useful it's going to be. Still, if it stops a few people from replying to messages and being lured into the trap, it'll have been worth it. The paper decided to keep it fairly cryptic."

"I see," said Bruce, knowingly, "Well, it's not 'cryptic, as you put it, anymore: Frank has only gone and distributed that video round all the major outlets. He's called me personally to tell me about it. I think he's only done it in the past half hour, so it'll take some time for it to hit the airwaves...but when it does you better be ready for a reaction; I'm not sure what it's going to be yet, this is unknown territory, but something's going to happen—could be mass hysteria to mass ridicule, to anything in between."

Bruce had stayed away from the other key issue: the reaction of the Shaz. It was pretty clear that they were going to have access to what was happening, albeit with a bizarre interpretation of things. Would they punish the people that they were holding, or was it possible that they would let them go?

"There's something else," he continued, "We got another batch of images this morning and it looks like your friend Doob is right when he said that there were thousands more captures planned, we've got images of the same thing, empty cubes but clearly they're there for some reason."

Included in the mail that they had received from the Shaz had been more footage of new 'recruits' in the same strange role of 'transferring' knowledge via headphones. There had also been a lot more pictures of bodies, with the word 'reject' pinned onto the front; the message was in a variety of languages, leading to the assumption that they had been left in the places that they had been taken from—places across the globe.

Ellie had stayed quiet but she was clear about what she thought the right course of action was, now that things had taken such a dramatic twist.

"I think we should all be together," she said, half to Bruce and the others in Edinburgh and half to Ravi. "Whatever happens now, it's likely to be important, if not decisive and perhaps this is exactly what we need to get in and see the Shaz, and then we can try to end this, once and for all.

Ravi agreed. In his heart he felt that *he* was the only one that had the responsibility for trying to resolve things. He knew that it was his destiny to try and meet with the Shaz, on their ground and finish this once and for all. Sure, there might be a plethora of agencies offering theories on everything from 'nuking' them, to trying to create a new society of us and them living harmoniously together—but he knew that he would have to find a way to stop the

Shaz.

"I agree with you Ellie. We have to be prepared for whatever happens next *together.*"

NO HIDING PLACE

Ravi and Ellie spent the evening partly preparing to go back to Scotland, partly saying a (hopefully) temporary goodbye to Angel and Doob and partly keeping an eye on the reaction to the release of the footage by Frank Tobin. It was several hours later that the first reaction started to roll through.

At first there was just the slightest murmurings—some news wires with reports that they were in receipt of un-corroberated footage, apparently showing mass kidnappings by what were 'unidentified' people (there was a general consensus to steer away from anything that deliberately named the 'people' as not human—these were serious news organisations, after all). As links started being made to recently missing people around the world and comments made that some of these people had been verified as having been the people shown murdered, the level of interest started to escalate.

Within the news rooms themselves, there was quite a bit of debate. Who was this 'Frank Tobin' and how had he got his hands of this bizarre footage. How authentic was it? Chiefs had scoured round a little and had found that the UK Tribune was already running a watered-down story, which seemed to have some additional information about how to avoid being a 'victim' of what they called a scam...but, from the look of the images, was abduction by weird small aliens.

The wires carried the stories as a bit of a public interest, slightly sick humour story to start with, after all there *were* bodies involved but to link them to being abducted by aliens...'give me a break' as editor after editor said. The early notification consisted of still pictures of the Shaz with comments about 'Photo-shop' and April Fools hoaxes (despite it being winter). There was a great deal of reluctance to spin the story any other way. Editors called other editors and reached the conclusion that, probably, the UK Tribune line was a good one to go down. Tony Ferrante became unreachable by phone; all questions were being taken by Ms Woods and the paper's legal team.

At some point during the day, someone, somewhere decided to run the actual footage on their website. That is when it started to become really interesting. Almost immediately, people's appetite for the story, already having been wetted by earlier and sketchier reports, went ballistic. Most of the sites crashed, as millions of people tried simultaneously to see what the fuss was about. Neighbours had alerted neighbours and social media was completely dominated by only one trending topic: aliens were on their way to taking over the planet. Memes instantly started to appear depicting the Shaz as, variously, benevolent friends or violent aggressors going around murdering people and committing grotesque acts of depravity.

Very few people actually believed that the Shaz were real aliens, of course. It was all a tremendous joke that everyone could join in. Initial TV broadcasts included humorous updates on the phenomenon that was sweeping the globe.

As the day wore on, however, some people began to look more seriously at the footage, watching it over and over again, pausing and rewinding, and zooming in, so that they could have a closer look at the people involved. It was assumed that all the people in the footage had been actors but there started to be rumours that actually they weren't, that maybe the bodies really were bodies...

Police forces around the world started taking an interest and called the Metropolitan Police in London, commenting that some of the people held a remarkable resemblance to people that they knew to be missing; relatives had come forward and were absolutely certain that they were the people that they knew. All of the people had gone missing fairly recently—within the past few months. The regional police force in Sao Paolo, Brazil, insisted that they were pretty sure that the woman lying dead in one of the images was a Victoria Gloria Romerez: a thirty-four year old government worker.

Later reports stopped treating the story as a joke. Opinion started to become split along two lines. The first was that this was an elaborate terrorist plot, kidnapping people at random anywhere in the world, with the only motive being to cause widespread panic and global fear (as this was what was beginning to transpire, if correct, this was proving to be a very effective strategy). The second was that this really was extra-terrestrials of some sort (or possibly a forgotten race of people who had acquired special powers) who were picking off people at will and who would not stop until they had taken over the world. As lurid tales emerged of possible sightings, instead of being dismissed as it had been earlier, this second explanation grew in popularity, and worldwide 'experts' started to appear on the twenty-four hour rolling news to give their opinion on just what the creatures were and what their intentions (past kidnapping and killing innocent people) might be.

One of the experts being called upon to give his opinion was Bruce. Fortunately for him Frank Tobin had not, as yet, given out Bruce's name as being 'of special interest' in connection to the odd creatures on the footage, however Bruce felt that it would only be a matter of time before Frank was directing attention and most probably blame, knowing Frank, his way. At the moment though, Bruce was in much demand by news channels worldwide to give his opinion, especially since the creatures in question seemed to be very similar in appearance to some that he claimed to have seen in the mid 1990s: an event that appeared to have initiated his interest in the subject and that he mentioned briefly in his academic paper "Living with the Alien'. So far Bruce had declined to comment, other than to say that it was worth taking the advice of Ben Rogers in the UK Tribune seriously: DO NOT respond to messages sent offering the chance to go on teaching assignments, unless you personally know the people or organisation sending the message.

Safely shut away from the media, in Juniper Green, the McLeish's waited for Ravi and Ellie to return to Edinburgh, watching footage on twenty-four hour news, liaising with their contact in the US SETUrity division and reading emails from journalists and other people that had started to find their way to Bruce and Elspeth's mailboxes. This was not because they were bored and wanted something to do; the individual stories might continue to give some clues about just how and why the Shaz had taken people.

Emails from the families had been particularly difficult to read. A man in St Ives, Cornwall, wrote to say that his wife, a modernist artist, had gone missing from their cottage; shortly beforehand she had called him about a new challenge she was thinking about....her husband had never managed to discover what this was to be. A taxi driver from Cairo emailed Bruce, pleading that he knew that his son had been taken by 'them'—his boy, a local college student was always online, he said; his son had just been accepted into a top university to study medicine, the email continued—he had his whole life in front of him and he would not have just disappeared. A teacher from Iowa in the US wrote that her partner had been discovered dead at the bottom of a ravine in Yellowstone National Park; he was a keen explorer and would never have put himself at any risk, she insisted. There had been a note attached to his clothing that she had seen and felt really disturbed by.

The growing number of missing people that were being found dead could not be ignored. Sure, the number of people that went missing *anyway*, before all of this, was far higher than most people ever appreciate, but the number of people who went missing and were then found dead within days or weeks was not normal. Nor was the fact that there was no immediate cause of death identifiable and that each victim was 'labelled' as a reject. Surely one group could not be acting in all the remote locations involved. Panic started to spread.

The McLeish's had been been in regular communication with the Secret Extra-terrestrial Unit in the US. SETU had been observing any unusual activity or sightings for decades. They had their own hi-tech observation facility, deep in the Utah desert and maintained cryogenically preserved specimens of possible extra-terrestrials in their bio-labs. SETU operated, relatively undisturbed, working off data supplied by thousands of amateur UFO spotters around the world, as well as university departments, meteorological offices and defense facilities. The Unit was seen, even by some of its own staff as a rather expensive gimic sometimes; it was not as if the billions invested in it over the decades had actually *resulted* in anything, past allowing a few grown up boys the opportunity to continue being obsessed with an unlikely fantasy. Almost overnight things had changed.

Instead of Bruce calling into SETU by video-link, SETU now called into the McLeish's—in dramatic style. Holed up inside the detached house on the outskirts of Edinburgh, Bruce, Matt and Elspeth were examining the results of the lab reports that had finally come back from Switzerland concerning the finger tissue samples, they made interesting reading and contained a number of anomalies that Elspeth was trying to figure out. They circled key readings and wrote question marks alongside them.

"These are, well, odd," said Elspeth, looking at the figures, "I'm sure that those readings are very different from the one's I took a few years ago...but it's from the same sample set. I can't understand it."

Their deliberations were interrupted by a loud sound out side the house. The sound appeared suddenly and was like a huge engineering works firing up around their house. The three of them immediately wondered whether it was the Shaz, although it did seem a bit odd that their arrival was quite so noisy this time. Then Bruce realised what it was.

"That's a helicopter, Elle," he said—moving over to the window, "There's a helicopter landing in our back garden."

They all moved over to look and, sure enough, at the far end of the large and manicured garden in Juniper Green, a black helicopter—the sort that might be used as an air ambulance, hovered for a while, its blades whirring loudly and methodically, forcing the McLeish's shrubs to flatten in submission. In the cockpit they could see three men, one in a flight uniform and the other two in black suits, they were both wearing dark glasses and looked for all the world like secret service agents.

"I don't think they're from round here," Elspeth said as the helicopter hovered over their garden.

A few feet off the ground, the men wearing suits jumped out of the aircraft onto the lawn and the other guy threw down a bag. Then, one of the men in the garden made a circular movement above his head with his finger instructing the pilot to leave and the helicopter ascended, then swooped away, the characteristic rhythmic clattering of its blades gradually fading.

Matt, Bruce and Elspeth stood framed in the picture window looking out onto the back garden as the tall, burly, immaculately dressed men wearing dark glasses walked purposefully towards them.

"I guess we better let them in," said Bruce as one of the visitors held up an official looking badge with the image of an Eagle in the background, "I think this is our man from SETU."

Brandon Curtis turned out to be a quite a nice chap, they

concluded as they shared a pot of tea, partly to get over the shock of the dramatic arrival. They'd communicated in written messages for some time, as he'd been one of the small number of contacts that Bruce had at SETU, but, as with quite a few people with an interest in the field, he'd not really given them much of a clue about his personality. His colleague, Carl, said very little, he appeared to be more of a minder figure and stayed very much in the background, whilst Brandon did the talking. Brandon and Carl looked distinctly out of place in the well-worn but elegant surroundings of the McLeish's old house

"I'm gonna get right into things," said Brandon as he stood up next to the monitor, his white teeth flashing as he spoke, "You know why I'm here and you know we need to do something fast. I've got authorisation from my superiors to share our strategy. We believe that the current situation presents a significant risk to national SETUrity and also to global SETUrity."

Brandon's American accent seemed out of place in the traditionally furnished room with its nick-nacks and rather higgledy piggledy furniture, his muscular physique and tanned, healthy look did not chime with the reality of a bleak Scottish winter. Brandon tripped over the edge of a rug as he paced up and own delivering his message. He was clearly more used to working in a shiny, spacious office, surrounded by hi-tech equipment.

"I'm here to do an initial assessment. This will probably take about two days," he spoke in a well-rehearsed way. "We'll let SETU take it from there...You guys, will, of course come with me back to the States, if we need your further assistance."

The McLeish's glanced at each other and Bruce raised one eyebrow as he spoke. "Hold on just a minute there Brandon. We're, as far as we know, the only people that these things have approached without a view to capturing as prisoners. We've been *chosen* as some sort of channel to speak to them and I'm not sure that we can just go along with anything you say like that..." His words were obviously falling on deaf ears as Brandon was accessing some media that he flashed up onto the monitor.

The screen showed, first of all, a compilation of bodies that bore the hallmarks of being victims of the Shaz, together with the names of the victims shown and some information about them. The victims shown were all based in the United States, Canada, or South America and it was stressed that several had roles that made them likely targets, based on their contribution to national life.

"Daniel Green was a high-school football player and mentor in his school," the voice-over stated, "He was earmarked for inclusion in the fast-track Ivy League Program. We think this is why he was chosen..." and so on.

The film went on through a few more examples and then broadened out to look at the impact around the globe. It noted the acceleration of the abductions and then stated the view of SETU that the prognosis for the abductees was not good. The film did refer to Ben's article and the idea that some sort of message relating to teaching was being used as a lure, however, it concluded that this was not something that they could agree was the way that people were being accessed. In the view of SETU it was more likely that people were abducted whilst they slept and were 'transported' up to a mother ship for processing, after which they assumed some sort of knowledge transferral role, as described in the video sent to Ben and others.

"It is highly likely that the extra-terrestrials are trying to access intelligence by harvesting the thoughts of people who they think may have key SETUrity information," continued the voice-over. "The extra-terrestrials will most likely be looking to exploit this information to overcome and subdue earth's inhabitants. The ultimate objective may be to colonise earth. We are treating the capture and murder of civilians as an act of aggression and feel that we are on the verge of being at war with the aliens."

Brandon stopped the film and waited for a while to allow the gravity of the last statement to sink in.

"What that means," he said looking around the room, "Is that we are getting ready to deploy our defences. I am here to establish whether you can help us."

"When you say 'deploy your *defences'* what exactly do you mean?" quizzed Bruce. "You know it could be extremely dangerous to use force against these things: they could react very unpredictably." He knew as well as Brandon and Carl that using any sort of force would escalate the amount of bloodshed. The difference was that SETU saw this as resulting in victory for the human race, whereas Bruce was not certain.

"Would it not be better to see if you could negotiate with the Shaz, as we are calling them?" said Elspeth, "Matt and I have done some analysis of their behaviour and we think that, if we could get to speak to them one to one, we could negotiate with them. They seem to be pretty uncertain of themselves sometimes; we think that we could find a way to get through to them."

Brandon said that that was exactly why he had come to see them; to establish if there were any other options...and to get information about where the extra-terrestrials were based.

"We don't want to have to send one soldier in unnecessarily, or deploy one missile" he said, "But it is the duty of SETU to advise and take instructions from leaders around the world in order to protect the human race. We are in contact with those leaders and they have committed themselves to acting together to protect the future of the world's people, if necessary.

"You mean they've got their nuclear weapons at the ready?" suggested Bruce.

"I'm not obliged to share that information with you, Sir," said

Brandon, "But we need your help to locate these aliens. If you do not assist us, it will delay our mission and many more people will die. Will you help us, Sir ?"

BACK UP NORTH

The world was gripped by a sense of helpless terror. The number of 'rejects' had increased dramatically: to the point where they were being counted in the hundreds rather than in the tens. How soon, thought Ravi would it be before they were counted in the millions?

Ravi and Ellie had arrived back in Scotland to the unusual scene of reporters outside Bruce and Elspeth's home and two strange American guys, looking for all the world like they'd stepped straight out of some federal agent clothing store, stationed inside it. Bruce had told them not to say too much to Brandon or Carl until they had properly spoken to each other.

There was hardly any time to absorb what was going on. The TV showed pictures of panicked families holding up pictures of loved ones with the word 'missing' as a caption. Walls had been created, plastered in photos of people who may have been taken. Lists started to emerge with descriptions of people who had been 'rejected' but had not been identified. Normal life had stopped.

Even though people were heeding the advice not to answer any messages sent to them by people they did not know, the number of people being taken had only escalated. Perhaps they had been wrong about the way that people were identified and abducted after all?

They had received messages from the Shaz. Always brief comments such as 'This is not fair', 'We need more time' and 'People are not playing well' They had tried asking what the messages meant, but none of their questions was ever replied to. Ravi and the others started feeling like they were on a wild goose chase. What was the point of maintaining their stand that things could be sorted out diplomatically, when it seemed increasingly obvious that they were being played as the fool? The day following Ravis and Ellie's return, whilst Brandon and Carl were engaged in talking to SETU headquarters Bruce called a hasty meeting to discuss their options.

"Look, I'm beginning to feel that the nuclear option is the right one now," said Bruce to the assembled team, "We can't justify people losing their lives."

"I agree," said Ravi. He thought about the images of bodies piling up in morgues in London, how long before one of them was Ellie's—or even his own? It was clear that the vague connection with himself that was a pre-requisite for being chosen by the Shaz was now redundant: the Shaz had made a connection from him to everybody else on earth. "Somehow we have to find them and destroy them, before they destroy us."

The others agreed, somewhat reluctantly. Elspeth and Matt still thought that there was a good chance that there was something missing and said that they would carry on looking; the results from the analysis of the finger continued to intrigue them. Bruce was initially dismayed that they might have to join forces with people intending to destroy the unique creatures, but it was becoming clear that, unless they were stopped, the scale of the destruction could be massive.

"I'm going to agree with helping SETU with their plans—I don't think we've got many options now, said Elspeth, "but, I honestly don't think that the Shaz know what they are doing: I don't think that they *realise* the damage that they are causing."

"That's insane, ma'am," said Brandon, who, unobserved by the others, had walked into the room. "Have you seen the number of dead bodies coming out from wherever they are? Are you telling me that this isn't a calculated plot of terror and destruction? I'm sorry, lady, but you've got it all wrong."

Elspeth didn't say anything. Perhaps the tall American was right, she thought to herself. Perhaps her gut instincts were wrong and the Shaz really were nasty, cruel and ruthless aliens. But then their messages always seemed so naïve and confused...innocent even.

"Besides," continued Brandon, "Why are they hiding out? If they don't think that killing us all is wrong, why not just park up and let us know where they are? You only hide if you know that you're hiding for a reason—that reason being that they know we'll fight back if we know where they are. We don't even know what part of the universe they are from"

This *did* make sense, thought Ravi: he had tried desperately to get the Shaz to reveal who they were over the past few weeks and they had never let on.

"I'm gonna have to report back to my superiors," said Brandon to the group. "I need to know: are you with us, or are you with the aliens?"

The group thought for a while. The scale of destruction had become too much.

"We're with you," they replied, somewhat reluctantly. The decision had been made. Ravi and the others were now involved in a race to locate and destroy the Shaz. Attention shifted to how to find them.

Over in the headquarters of SETU, in Utah, a collection of defence representatives from around the world had gathered to authorise the most critical defence campaign in the history of the human race. Around the oval board table, representatives from the world's great nations sat listening to Gerry Stukmeyer, President of SETU, as he talked through predictive statistics. The abductions were now occurring at a rate that suggested that a million people could be abducted within a period of approximately four weeks. Within a few months the entire planet could be decimated.

The delegates debated whether the aim of the aggressors was territorial: did they want to capture the earth to occupy it as a homeland? Gerry did not know the answer to this but said it was likely, based on their initial analysis of behavioural indicators, that this was the case. He was asked whether the aliens were abducting more people proportionally from one country or region than elsewhere. He replied that, whilst there was an early bias towards the United Kingdom, this seemed to have disappeared and current measures showed no particular location that had more people being taken. He added that there appeared to be no preference for male or female victims and that most victims seemed to be between the ages of ten and sixty years old.

Delegates paused from the discussion to watch a short broadcast showing the impact on life on earth. Communities were quickly becoming paralysed with fear. Even though, as a proportion of people on earth, the number of abducted was still relatively low, the impact of the totally unpredictable nature of the abductions had resulted in an unparalleled level of terror. The Shaz had kept sending short videos of themselves to media outlets, looking for all the world like they were oblivious to the impact of their actions. They always appeared in small groups, looking rather nervous and even appearing to try to smile towards the viewer. In their videos they said very little, apart from the fact that they were returning more 'rejects'.

Parents had very quickly stopped their children from going to school, but now people were, themselves, stopping away from work. Essential public services were just about being maintained as governments worldwide insisted that public servants carried on working and brought the military to keep services going. Power was starting to become a problem, systems were no longer being properly maintained, so any municipal problem was not routinely resolved and the knock on effect became cumulative. Hospitals were given priority. Then, as more and more homes lost power, people in the northern hemisphere (where it was winter) were forced to move to large communal shelters where they could have safety in numbers and some degree of basic nutrition and warmth. Back in the neighbourhoods that they had come from, looting became a problem, with gangs of young men roaming the streets with weapons. The world had become an apocalyptic place to be.

Through it all, people continued to be taken. No-one knew how (Ravi remained convinced that the original method for entrapping people involved the use of messages on the internet, but this now appeared to be irrelevant). It could be that the Shaz had, as with their choice of victims, loosened the criteria. It was now possible, for example, that just by entering a site or accessing a common page, people became potential victims. No one seemed to have witnessed anyone being abducted.

The broadcast was paused and Gerry Stukmeyer returned to his lectern.

"You can see, ladies and gentlemen, just how important it is that we find and destroy these things. Even without the worst case scenario, humanity stands to regress to a point of almost no return pretty quickly given the numbers of people on earth. Can you imagine what's going to happen if the situation worsens in China say; the number of people involved?"

None of the delegates were under any illusions about the gravity of the situation, neither, for once, did any representative feel that their national interests were divorced from those of any other person in the room.

"There appear to be two main problems," said Martha Felix, the British representative, "Firstly, we don't know if our defences are any use against these aliens at all and, secondly we don't know where the hell they are!"

The audience rumbled in agreement. How, if they didn't even know *where* the aggressor was, were they going to be able to do anything at all? How could they fight an invisible enemy?

"Well," said Gerry knowingly...he cleared his throat. "We have, for the first time got a firm indication of the whereabouts of the extra-terrestrials—and they're not too far from you, Martha."

Martha Felix looked apprehensive; a major deployment of nuclear weapons above the United Kingdom was not exactly a welcome prospect.

"Well, we know from our agents in Scotland: Curtis and Turner, that a small group of the aliens has visited an area close to Edinburgh, possibly on more than one occasion." He gestured to a colleague at the side of the room to come forward with a notebook. He read it out carefully to the surprised delegates:

"We can confirm that the aliens have made previous contact with the McLeish family in Edinburgh, Scotland and a group of them appear to have established themselves near to the family, at a location called Bonnybridge. The aliens have made no demands and appear to be ready to talk to a member of the group."

"Ladies and Gentlemen," he said, slowly. "Once the main location of the enemy has been confirmed we can prepare the attack."

Back in Juniper Green things had, of course, taken a few twists.

After their decision to assist in the elimination of the Shaz, a decision they were not completely sure was the right one, Ravi and Ellie had a brainwave: why didn't they go back to the location on the 'road to nowhere' where they had appeared before? After all, they had already appeared there, so this had to be their best chance of seeing them by far. Ravi and Ellie talked to the others and debated whether to let Brandon and Carl in on their plans. Bruce and Elspeth no longer saw the Shaz as harmless and insisted that, if Ellie and Ravi were going to attempt a meeting, they should all go along. Matt, who had never seen the Shaz, insisted on going along too. With no time to lose, it was decided that they would just 'take a punt' and go to the location, hoping that the Shaz would just turn up, as before. They couldn't really exclude Brandon and Carl, so they would have to come too.

Within a couple of hours, the whole party had got ready and set off for the potential meeting point. They drove in a convoy of three vehicles to the familiar location. Ravi went with Ellie in her car. About a mile behind, Elspeth, Bruce and Matt followed them in the Land-Rover. Brandon and Carl followed up the rear in a hired black saloon car.

En route, Ellie and Ravi discussed how they would react if by a stroke of 'luck' they met with the Shaz—they described it as luck in an ironic way, as they knew that there was a chance that they would also be abducted. They no longer trusted the small, rather clumsy looking creatures and would remain vigilant to any 'tricks'. Their plan was to try to persuade the Shaz into telling them where they were based and where they were holding their victims. Any additional information would be a bonus. Persuading the Shaz—*if* they showed up of course—was not likely to be easy, however Ellie had a good idea.

"Look, Ravi, they seem to be treating things as some sort if game, right? That's the way they've always talked in the messages. Well, why don't you say that you need to play the game with them back on their ship? I don't know... just say that its a new rule or something."

Ravi thought that this plan sounded very unlikely to fool the Shaz, after all they were a species that seemed to be able to exert some sort of mind control over people and magic them away, without anyone knowing how they did it. However, he didn't want to discourage Ellie and, besides, he didn't have any ideas of his own.

"It sounds worth a shot," he replied.

Their car drew close to the spot where they had 'met' the Shaz a few weeks earlier—there was the road-sign with its familiar red triangle. Looking behind them, into the slight mist, they could see the headlights of the Land-Rover. Then the headlights went off, as agreed, to minimise the disruption.

"Well, what now?" asked Ellie.

The couple sat on the wall, talking very quietly and looking around nervously. The cold seemed to clear the head and Ravi found himself speaking out loud as he tried to make sense of the pieces of the jigsaw puzzle. Some elements of the puzzle had kept going round and round in his mind and, for some reason, this seemed to be a good time to offload them.

"Ellie, doesn't it strike you as odd that the Shaz haven't made any demands?" said Ravi quietly, "I mean they haven't even said anything *that* threatening."

"I guess so," said Ellie, "but then again actions speak louder than words, I suppose."

"And you remember when you first met with them, when you were a child, they said that Bruce and Elspeth could be part of the *solution.* Since then, they keep talking as if they are looking for a solution to *something.* I mean, even calling the people that they take their 'friends'. It's almost like they want our help, or people's help for something, but they start bumping them off when they can't deliver—it's like we've let *them* down...like we're the bad guys."

"You mean when they dump people with the label 'reject', it's like we've delivered faulty goods to them or something?"

"Exactly," said Ravi.

"But, how come they don't tell us what they're trying to solve?" said Ellie, "If they want our help why not just ask us for it, rather than grabbing people and killing them for no reason?...and how is it all connected to you anyway, Ravi? I mean, don't take this the wrong way, but why not the President of the United States, or the Chinese Premier...or even some corporate magnate, surely those people make more sense that latching onto a schoolboy from London?"

Ravi had to agree that he did seem like a pretty unlikely choice as the inter-galactic 'chosen-one' of a species of short, humanoid creatures but, then again, why not? he asked himself...perhaps the Shaz thought he had special powers; perhaps he *did* have special powers! He was brought rudely back to earth by Ellie's pragmatism

"Perhaps they mistook you for someone else: someone important."

"Thanks," said Ravi, sarcastically.

It was at that moment that they saw something. Ellie knew what it was, instantly .

THE NEXT ENCOUNTER

Seemingly appearing out of nowhere, the same small flying saucer shape balanced on the walls, just as it had all those years ago. Behind them, Ravi and Ellie could here footsteps; Bruce Elspeth and Matt were keeping a discreet distance away.

"Just watch that space," said Ellie, pointing towards a spot on the base of the spacecraft.

Sure enough, a door opened and a Shaz slid down a chute to join them and then another. Ravi thought just how comical they looked...but then he remembered just how deadly they were proving to be.

The two Shaz, one male and one female stood on their small legs looking towards them.

"We have come here," said the female Shaz.

"They're always stating the bloody obvious," whispered Ellie, "Try and find out where they are holed up!"

"Just let me do things in my own way," Ravi snapped back; he'd been thinking about a new approach

"Thank you for being here," he said stepping a little closer to the Shaz. "I have been waiting to speak to you."

"We have been waiting to speak to you," said the male Shaz.

Ravi could hear one set of footsteps drawing closer to them along the road and wondered who it was.

"We are disappointed, Ravi."

"I know, I am sorry," replied Ravi.

"We thought that you were going to give us more help to learn and more clues...like you said..." The Shaz looked visibly rather upset and agitated.

"Like I said?" repeated Ravi, perplexed. The footsteps behind him had stopped, he looked around a little and saw Matt standing a little to the side; he was the only one who had not seen the Shaz in 'person' out of the five of them in the team, and he had felt a little short-changed.

"Yes, Ravi. We have been trying to find the answers and find the clues, but we have not been able to succeed very much. We have returned the rejects to you."

"We have noted that," said Ravi, trying to think what they could mean.

"Hey, I'm a friend of Ravi's," Matt piped up, stepping forward so that they could see him. "How's it going?"

Ravi gave Matt a glare. "Get, back," he snarled, it might not be safe."

"Don't worry dude," said Matt, "I'm cool with them."

"How is what going?" asked the female Shaz.

Matt approached the Shaz with his usual slow sauntering walk. "Y'know...that's just how people talk, dude... I say to you 'how's it going'—its just a way of talking. It means 'hiya', is everything OK? —that sort of thing." Matt thought for a while and then added, "Like, if I say to you everything's 'cool', I don't literally mean that everything is at a cold temperature: what I mean is that everything is fine, things are going well. D'you get me?...I mean, do you understand?"

The Shaz turned to each other and whispered together for some time. They looked as if they were discussing something of some importance, or coming to some sort of decision. Ravi and Ellie slowly walked up to join Matt, closer to the space-ship and the Shaz. Finally the Shaz spoke.

"We are interested in what you are saying," the Shaz said, pointing a stubby hand at Matt, "We would like to learn more about this way of speaking."

"Hold on a minute," said Ravi anxiously, remembering the Shaz's apparent preferred style of learning, "No-one's gonna be hooked up to those headphones: we've seen what happens to those people."

The Shaz again talked together quietly, they seemed to be agitated about something.

"I like your ship..." Matt called over, deciding to try to change the subject, "It's really cool."

He had decided to try to give the Shaz, since they were so interested in street talk, a little bit of informal practice. "To be honest, guys 'cool' is a pretty old fashioned way of talking now, I'm too old and geeky to know what the *real* kids are saying nowadays. When I was at school it went from 'bad' to 'phat', 'safe', 'ballin'...It could be something completely different now. D'you get me...?" Matt was really quite enjoying himself.

The Shaz looked over at Matt with great interest. They seemed perplexed, but at the same time quite fascinated and interested in this strange concept that you could actually express yourself by using words that seemed to have nothing whatsoever to do with what you were saying.

"What you are saying is of interest to us," suggested the female Shaz, nodding appreciatively towards Matt. "We have not encountered this phenomenon before, when speech does not correlate with meaning."

"We will need to investigate this," agreed the other creature

Though Ravi was intrigued by all of this chit-chat, he was also a little annoyed that valuable time was being wasted when what they really needed was to find out where the Shaz were hiding out, so that they could help the SETU mission to save the world. Firstly, there was the pressing need to, if at all possible, save the existing abductees and, secondly, the 'big one'—eliminating the Shaz. Although it seemed that things had now got to the stage where military action seemed inevitable, part of Ravi (and the rest of the team) still hoped that they might be able, somehow, to stop killing people and get the Shaz to just leave.

"We appreciate your interest in our ways," he said, deciding to try the polite approach. "We can see that you like to learn—to acquire knowledge," he continued cautiously, an idea building in his mind, "I know that you are learning from people that are with you, in your home."

"They have not been very helpful," said the Shaz, regretfully, "We have had to send some of them back and are getting replacements."

"Well, we want you to stop taking those people. You need to return those people, the ones you have taken, because, for us, this is a very serious issue and is leading to a lot of problems. People are getting very angry about it."

The Shaz looked quite perplexed by this. "No, Ravi. We can't do that, it would be against the rules. You know that."

"What rules...why do you keep going on about rules?" shouted Ravi, getting frustrated, "Don't you see that you are murdering people? This isn't a game...you need to stop now, or we will fight back!"

"Oh, but it *is* a game" said the Shaz...clapping his little hands childishly, "It's *your* game. You set the game and since then you have been no fun! We are getting a bit bored with things now, Ravi, we are really not happy..."

This is bizarre, thought Ravi, The capture of all those people was sick anyway but to be part of a *game* and not only a game but 'his' game...

"OK," he said, "If it is my game I'm not playing any more, so please stop, let those people go and just leave."

"No!" the answer was blunt and stubborn. "The game doesn't end like that."

Ravi slumped his shoulders and looked despairingly towards Ellie. Her forehead was scrunched up, like she had been concentrating hard on the interchange and had been trying to make sense of it. Her look back at Ravi told him that she had not been able to get very far.

"Hey, guys, can we have a look around your ship?" Matt called out, pointing at the space-craft behind them, "I'd love to have a ride in it."

What was Matt trying to do, thought Ravi, did he have a plan or was he just being curious?

The Shaz looked pleased. They quite liked this stubbly man, with his strange way of talking. He looked as if he wanted to be their friend. The Shaz talked for a while in their strange, croaky language.

"We would like you to join us in our craft and we will take you..." said the female Shaz, she looked at her colleague and said a few words in their unintelligible language, she seemed to be checking something with him, "...for a ride," she continued. Matt thought that he even detected a hint of a smile from her towards him.

"Great," said Matt, walking forward, "Lets go! Hold on...can these guys come too?" he gestured towards Ravi and Ellie.

"Hold on Matt," said Ravi frantically, trying to whisper, "We just want enough information to give SETU—not to get captured by the Shaz ourselves and found on some street with tags on our chests!"

"That's not what's gonna happen, bro...I don't know why but I think we'll be OK with these guys. I've just got a hunch about it...Anyway have you got a better plan?"

The Shaz said that it was acceptable that Ravi and Ellie joined Matt.

"Hey," said Matt, "That sounds great. The only thing is, we need to come back here after say thirty minutes. Will you bring us back after that time and leave us here?....and none of those headphones and shit, we're just interested in going for a ride , yeah."

"Yes, we will," said the Shaz, looking sincere.

"Matt could be right," agreed Ellie, "I haven't detected any sign of aggression towards us at all from them."

Ravi could see that he had no choice.

"Well, it looks like the three of us are coming on board," said Matt, "Just tell us what to do."

"Hold on just one minute there," Bruce's voice sounded out, as he appeared out of the shadows into the pool of light made by the space-craft.

"Yes, you three are going nowhere," added Elspeth joining him. "Do you really think that we can let you go off on your own?

Ellie had already thought that her grandparents would not take easily to the idea of leaving her with the Shaz.

"Elspeth, we need someone here, don't you see?" she protested, "You'll be no help if we run into trouble if you're with us. We need you and Bruce to stay here and monitor what's going on. Hopefully, we'll only be gone for a very short time anyway."

Elspeth and Bruce did not look at all convinced by Ellie's argument. They had always been very liberal guardians, but leaving Ellie to fly off with an alien species who had already kidnapped and killed scores of people...well, that was a different kettle of fish.

Just as a whispered argument between the three of them was ensuing, two burly figures also walked out into the light: two men dressed in black suits and wearing dark glasses even though it was now night.

"We cannot allow this mission to go ahead without our presence," said Brandon with his American drawl, "We need an affirmative for us becoming part of the mission...That means we want to come along," he added.

There was getting to be quite a queue.

The Shaz were, understandably, a little surprised by the appearance of so many new people and were starting to look a bit uncertain about the debate. After a quick discussion of their own, they decided to be generous.

"You can all come along, if Ravi and his friend agree," the female Shaz said invitingly, "We can accommodate you all."

"Just a few minutes," Ravi called to them from the huddle of people debating the best combination to board the ship. It all seemed suspiciously easy, he thought to himself: could it be part of a set-up? He looked across as the Shaz, who appeared a little irritated at the delay. Ravi decided that, set-up or not, they had to go on.

The Mcleishs and the Americans were adamant that they wanted to go along with Ellie, Ravi and Matt. Bruce and Elspeth were sure that they would be able to use their knowledge to identify significant features of the ship and analyse the occupants. They could also 'keep an eye' on the others, although the others thought that they were more than able to look after themselves.

Brandon and Carl said that they had 'orders' that if anything significant happened they *must* be included, if not lead the mission; they were the SETU representatives and needed access to any control systems that might be onboard. They had been trained in identifying hostile weapons systems and controls (which, admittedly, none of the others had a clue about) and therefore they would be far more useful in getting valuable military intelligence out of the mission. Although they were not sure what powers or weapons the Shaz used on an individual basis, they thought (correctly) that they would be the mostly likely to be able to overpower the Shaz based on just physical strength—although Ravi pointed out that this was likely not to be that great a strategy, given the circumstances.

Finally, it was agreed that Bruce and Elspeth would remain behind and Brandon and Carl would go along with the others. The McLeish's accepted the argument that it was, perhaps, better if someone remained to get help if things went wrong. Brandon and Carl were just not going to take no for an answer.

The Shaz looked relieved that a decision had been made and ushered the group towards the waiting craft. When everyone was standing below the door of the 'flying saucer' they were, one by one, seemingly 'sucked' upwards into the craft, suddenly bouncing into the body of the ship. The door shut. Bruce and Elspeth watched as the space-craft silently swooped to one side and disappeared.

On the craft, the party looked at each other and then around them with surprise. Brandon and Carl even took off their dark glasses, so that they could see their surroundings more clearly. Once the party was escorted onto the main 'deck', it was clear to them that the small ship *was* actually just a small ship, not the incredible tardis-like affair that they had imagined it to be.

About ten Shaz sat around a central control table, twiddling banks of buttons and dials and behind them were walls of flashing lights. It all looked quite old fashioned and more than a little 'Star-trek' to the group. There was a large monitor that showed a map of the world and some smaller monitors, one of which displayed a large blueish globe; the others were blank.

"This is interesting," said Ellie, "walking up to the monitors and looking at the blue image, "Is this your *home*?"

"No it is what you call..." the small Shaz, who appeared to be in charge of the monitors, stopped and confirmed a word with another Shaz, "...it's what you call a 'screen-saver'."

Ravi was watching the main screen intently. "Ellie, come back and look at this," he suggested.

Ellie walked back to where Ravi was standing and looked up. A plot was being tracked across the map, in the same way that you'd see the journey route being slowly traced on the seat monitors of a plane. The plot was moving north-westwards, crossing over what looked like Iceland and continuing its trajectory over the frozen wilderness of Greenland. The craft must have been going pretty damn fast, thought Ravi as within a few minutes they seemed to have reached their destination: an island off the western coast of Greenland.

"Is that another screen-saver?" asked Ellie of the female Shaz standing next to her, who looked as if she was guiding the ship with some sort of video game joystick.

"No," replied the Shaz..."We have come to visit our base."

Brandon looked carefully at the map and said something into the lapel of his jacket; he had not figured on being quite so lucky so early. The Shaz had voluntarily, it seemed, given them the exact co-ordinates of their target.

The door opened once again and the Shaz slid down the chute onto the frozen ground. Ravi, Ellie and the Americans followed but Matt said that he would rather stay on the warm ship in order to have a better look around and chat to the other Shaz. This seemed like a good idea, especially once the others realised just how cold it was on the island.

"I see you share your this feeling of *cold* that the others have," said the Shaz, offering them some blankets for warmth, "We don't have the need for these coverings. We have only to go across this bridge and we will be there, so you will not be at this temperature for very long."

The Shaz pointed ahead and there, camouflaged by the ice but now clearly visible, was a *huge* version of their small craft. It loomed above them, to a height of what must have been hundreds of metres, though they could not actually see past the overhang of the bay above. Along the white of its hull were dotted black portholes and flashing lights. Very 'Hollywood', thought Ravi; the craft certainly looked as if it would not have been out of place in a big budget science fiction movie.

The party was bundled inside by the Shaz, whilst the small ship remained sitting on the ice nearby, like a very, very small scale model of its big brother. Once inside the 'mother' ship, the sheer scale of the Shaz's operation became clear. Hundreds of the small creatures lined the circular decks of the ship, which were arranged in layers around the outside of the ship. Three Shaz wearing red robes were waiting to greet them and, though, apart from their clothing, there was no real difference in appearance between these Shaz and the others, there seemed to be some sort of hierarchy, with these guys at the top. The other Shaz stepped into the background and the new 'red' Shaz showed the group around. They didn't say much, preferring to communicate in gestures with the party, though they did talk amongst themselves in 'Shaz-speak'.

The decks were like a mini city with areas where the Shaz sat around talking, interspersed with other areas where they looked as if they were talking to others of their kind on the monitors (Ravi thought that the Shaz on the monitors looked a little different to the Shaz that they had met, but he couldn't quite put his finger on what the difference was...they were too far away for him to see clearly).

On some of the decks, the Shaz were engaged with gadgets and pieces of equipment that they appeared to be assembling: brightly coloured gizmos and machines, some of the objects equipped with lights and making strange sounds. They were obviously quite an industrious lot. The whole thing had the look and feel of a large shopping mall.

In one section of a deck Ravi spotted some familiar faces. There was a small area that looked, for all the world, like an open-plan café, similar to the kind that you might find in a mall, or a multiplex cinema. Sitting around chatting, on the tubular chrome chairs, were several *humans*—not Shaz. The group numbered five people and consisted of an old woman hunched over a magazine, a sophisticated oriental woman in a tailored suit and a tall African tribesman wearing a long white robe; the other two people in the group were a small Indian girl in a turquoise shalwar kameez and a swarthy man wearing an overcoat. I bet if I talked to him, he'd have an Eastern European accent, thought Ravi. The people in the group didn't look like they were prisoners; they seemed very relaxed and familiar with each other, the little girl skipped about giggling, seemingly very happy with her unconventional companions. Seeing that the group had caught Ravi's eye, the female 'uber' Shaz explained that these people were known to them as the 'ancestors'. It was clear that they had a special function, or place amongst the Shaz. The different fate of the captive abductees soon became abundantly clear.

The party looked down into the massive central courtyard area and the mood of the group, which had been up to that point fairly neutral, changed. In the central area was a honeycomb of small cells, arranged in layers with obscured walls. In some of the cells was the familiar sight of a person wearing headphones and a Shaz. These were the rooms that had been broadcast in the ominous images sent by the Shaz. They looked with horror at the arrangement, there must have been thousands of the cells, and Ravi noted that many of them were empty. He suddenly remembered that this was the reason that they were there; he remembered Doob and the almost lifeless state that he had been in—it was only through some amazing good fortune that he had not been delivered, like the others, with a tag on his chest. He realised that the Shaz were not some cuddly little aliens: they were the enemy.

Brandon and Carl had been looking around earnestly. Ravi guessed that they were sizing up the configuration of the ship, in terms of trying to rescue the prisoners. If there was no clear route to get them out, would they even bother storming the ship? thought Ravi, or would they just take it out complete with all the prisoners on board?

Ellie asked if they could be taken around one of the decks to have a look around but the Shaz were reluctant. They seemed wary of letting them have a closer look at the activities of their compatriots and, in particular, they were cagey about the media screens dotted about—the one's that the Shaz were communicating to their own kind on. Ravi thought that, from a distance, the images on the screens looked a little different to the Shaz around them...perhaps a bit more *mature*, shall we say.

The Shaz became a bit agitated at the enquires being made about them from members of the group and started to usher them back to the transport ship...Anyway, reminded the Shaz, they had to be getting back to meet the time restriction that they had been so concerned about. As if to reinforce this Ellie's mobile phone went off.

"Hello, Elspeth," she replied, rather embarrassed, "Yes we"ll be back in about ten minutes, I think, we've been on a bit of a journey..."

Back on the small transport craft, Matt had clearly been getting to know the Shaz a bit better and had struck up conversations with them, hoping to gain some insight into what the 'game' was and what made the Shaz 'tick'. He tried to establish whether the psychological analysis that Elspeth and he were building up matched what he saw and whether there were any clues relating to their weaknesses—weaknesses that people might be able to exploit in a confrontation. He had discovered a very interesting fact—one that solved the mystery of what the game was and why they were playing it.

The group was bundled off the main craft and over the narrow bridge back to the mini-craft. The small vessel then retraced the plot back to the small stretch of road in Falkirk, Scotland where Bruce and Elspeth were waiting. True to their word the Shaz let the party off the ship and even seemed to wave at them as their ship glided off into the night.

PREPARATION

Back at the house, the atmosphere was one of guarded exchanges. Everyone had their own views on the right course of action, despite the fact that they had all now signed up to destroying the Shaz.

Brandon took control. He had noted the location of the mother ship and he had already relayed this to SETU. They were briefing delegates and agreeing an international mission as he spoke, he said. He'd reviewed their apparent defence capabilities and it seemed that the ship would not withstand a direct hit. From what he had heard there was no backup and, if there was, it was a risk they had to bear, taking into account the fact that the Shaz had made it clear that they were not going to stop taking people, subjecting them to torture and killing them.

Brandon seemed convinced that the Shaz did not have another terrestrial base. Even if this was true, Elspeth reminded him, with the speeds they were capable of surely they would be able to launch an attack from anywhere very quickly? Brandon agreed that this may very well be the case, but he said that SETU command had agreed that their original mission to take out the base still stood, especially now that they knew where it was. I bet most of the delegates are men, thought Elspeth—all this macho stuff is not properly thought through and it's not going to get us anywhere.

Ravi sighed, he agreed with Brandon that a military solution did, after all, seem that the only way to end things, or at least the way to send the Shaz a message that they could not act with impunity. They had to try and rescue the prisoners and then take out the ship.

"We're still looking into what to do about the prisoners

onboard," admitted Brandon, "It complicates things quite a bit...I'm afraid there might be 'collateral damage."

"What on earth are you talking about," said Ellie, furiously, "have you people been playing too many video games or something...those are people not sandbags."

"One thing is agreed," said Bruce, trying to calm things down a little, "Whatever happens we need to act fast. The Shaz have said they are going to keep taking people. At the moment we know where they are but what's to say that by next week they may not have moved somewhere else; it would be different if they had a physical land base but that ship of theirs—it could go anywhere."

"Exactly, " agreed Brandon, "I've already made arrangements for all of you to go to Utah to the headquarters of SETU, just so you are away from danger in case they decide to retaliate by coming here. Not that we expect any retaliation: we're aiming for one hundred percent take out."

"Leave our home...you must be joking, pal," said Bruce. The others agreed that they were going nowhere.

Matt had stayed quiet up to that point, as he hadn't wanted to say too much to Brandon and Carl before he had consulted with the others, but now he felt that he had no choice. He wanted to stop any attack if he could and there might just be a way. There was a chance that he could land Ravi in it, but they were running out of time, so he had to just go for it.

"I think I know how this all started," he said quietly, "When you guys were on that big mother-ship out there, I got to asking about what they meant about this 'game' thing and how it all, like, started." Matt felt suddenly very self conscious.

All eyes in the room were on Matt. Ravi had been racking his brain since the start about why he, a completely innocuous young person from London, had become embroiled in the most critical incident in the modern history of the planet. Perhaps now he was going to find out.

"Well I asked the Shaz about the game and they said that Ravi —or Coolio345londonboy as they called him, sent them instructions for a game many years ago, and they've been preparing for it since then. Once they felt ready to play, they started collecting 'worthy opponents, as they put it...It seems like the opponents, weren't quite up to the job."

"Just how was Ravi...presumably then a schoolboy, going to accidentally send these aliens messages, when SETU and the top academics and scientists in the world had been getting nowhere with the same mission for decades?" asked Brandon, clearly annoyed with Matt's suggestion, "...and why the hell would their first contact with the human race be to play some sort of cockamany game?"

"Look, I can't give you the logic behind things, dude! I am just, like, telling you how it is...what I saw and heard on that ship. It's up to you to do something with it or not."

Ravi urged Matt to go on, he was sure that his friend would have found out something useful. As for Brandon et al....it looked as if they had already made their minds up anyway.

"When I talked to the Shaz," Matt continued, "They, like, told me, quite proudly actually, that the game was, like, *the* big thing in town. I asked them if I could have a look at the rules but then you guys came back and we all had to leave."

Brandon and Carl remained totally unconvinced. The fact that there was some 'game' being played made no difference to the fact that the Shaz were hostile aggressors—spinning this ridiculous story was just a way to pull the wool over everyone's eyes and move the focus away from the escalating level of killing. Aliens were smart, they said—especially when there were kids stupid enough to believe them. At that point, Brandon and Carl must have got some message through their ear-pieces, as they abruptly left the room, saying that they were needed for a report.

"Does any of this make any sense to you, Ravi...the game?" asked Ellie. "Think back to when you were at school. I matched that address to your school authority; did you do any sort of project in school that involved a game or something like that. Think Ravi...if we can work out what the game is about maybe we can finish it and the Shaz will go away."

Ravi thought and thought. He could not remember using the name Coolio345londonboy and neither could he remember any game. Ellie said that this was when he must have been in year ten or eleven; about the same time as when he had visited India. The whole idea of a game did seem to fit with the way that the Shaz had spoken: the stuff about the rules, it not being fair and so on...He knew that Matt had accurately told them what he had heard from the Shaz, but try as he might he could not remember anything about a game.

On the other side of the Atlantic, SETU was holding an emergency meeting. Brandon had sent through a load of images and co-ordinates from the main Shaz base. Gerry had the floor.

"As our agent says, we have also revealed the exact location of their main craft as being off the coast of Greenland, " he flashed a map over the screen. "I have already had the coast of Greenland surveyed and had picked up unusual readings coming from a location called 'Disko Oer'. This is the island identified as being the location of the alien base by out agent."

The one delegate representing the Scandinavian countries, including Denmark and Norway, the countries with the strongest economic and cultural claims over Greenland, started to protest strongly that he had not been consulted about this prior to the meeting.

"I know that, Sir," continued Gerry, " and I apologise. However we have just had this information in to us, within the past half-hour, and I think that when you see the finer details of agent Curtis's assessment, you'll realise that we don't have any time to lose."

The delegates looked on, horrified, at the pictures of the cube like structures of the 'hive'. Brandon gave his assessment by video-link.

"My view is that this is just the start, Sir," Gerry said respectfully to the Scandinavian delegate, "I believe that these things could easily be building similar premises *underneath* Greenland itself. We believe that we detected unusual readings on some of our instruments in the vicinity of the mother-ship."

"Did you receive any active threats," asked Martha Felix, "Were there any indications that these creatures are actively planning to kill more people?"

"Yes ma'am, that would be an affirmative," continued Brandon, "We heard them say that they were going to continue to replace people who are eliminated from the pods. Well, you can see that it won't take many rotations for that to become a serious issue, and we are just talking here about their existing punishment cells."

Martha looked downhearted, even though it was not Scotland, Greenland was still fairly close to the United Kingdom and any nuclear fallout could possibly affect the UK. Gerry reassured her that the island was on the opposite side of Greenland to the United Kingdom. Of course, this new location was of great concern to the Canadian delegate.

"Isn't there any way that we can deploy ground or conventional air forces rather than engage the nuclear option?" he asked, "We want to avoid both killing and long term damage to people and the environment, after all."

Canadians and their 'environmental' stuff thought Gerry. "Sorry, Sam...no can do...the nuclear option is the only one that would prevent any remaining aliens from contacting any of their kind for assistance. That reminds me, we'll have to send this Ravi guy out, with or without his friends, to get that little ship to the same location, otherwise there's gonna have to be another boom right over Edinburgh."

He reminded the delegates that their leaders had *already* agreed to the nuclear option in these circumstances; they had just been waiting for the location. Now, by this amazingly good fortune, they had that location. What were they waiting for?

Gerry anticipated that, with the preparations that they had already done, they could have missiles ready to be deployed by 1200 hours the next day, but would delay operations by a day to give people in affected areas time to evacuate their citizens to safe areas. Fortunately, the surrounding area was pretty sparsely populated and he was hoping that 'collateral damage' would be kept to a minimum. It was too risky to try to evacuate the people already on the base; all nations were represented there and he hoped that those lost would be remembered as heroes, he said.

The Canadian and Scandinavian delegates said that two days was, absolutely, not enough time to remove people from the area: some inhabitants in the regions could not even be contacted in two days, let alone leave to a safe area. Gerry insisted that this was the only way and that performing the operation swiftly would lead to the least panic worldwide. He reminded delegates how dire the situation on the ground was getting for the billions of people elsewhere in the world—the water and food shortages, looting, rapes and murders. What sort of society were they going to end up with if they didn't do anything?

The final vote was overwhelmingly in favour of taking action, as Gerry had predicted.

Brandon was continuing to speak in the background. He had decided that he needed to give them everything he knew—just in case anything went wrong, he didn't want to have to take the blame for an incomplete report. He was saying something about a kid and some sort of game. The delegates didn't hear him though, they were already on their phones and notebooks, following up on questions from the political leaders who had been hanging on to every word of the briefing.

Back in Scotland, Ravi was struggling to recall just when he could have sent anyone anything about a game. He thought carefully. When he was in year eleven how, exactly, did he use the name coolio345londonboy? He knew it was connected to school...could it have been connected to the business task through which he had contacted Victoria Romerez? Could it have something to do with a course in IT? His mind drew a blank...perhaps it was just some sort of joke amongst his friends, he thought, desperately. If it was, surely no one would remember. He was not even sure whether remembering the game would prove of any value to them anyway.

"Of course it will be," he said out loud to himself, "If you know how to win the game, you can end it."

He sat with a piece of paper with the words GAME and coolio345londonboy at the top. He then drew arrows from the words to anything that came to mind—subjects, people, events: nothing seemed to jump out as a solution.

In the rest of the house people had been briefed about the timing of the assault against the Shaz: they knew it was in less than two days. Apart from this they had been pretty much kept in the dark. They were neither encouraged to contact the Shaz, nor seemingly stopped from doing so. The atmosphere was that of a massive intake of breath: everyone seemed to be waiting for the next move. Whether out of a desire to find a last minute breakthrough to prevent the inevitable strike, or in the hope of discovering something—some weakness, that would mean that the Shaz could be comprehensively overcome, they beavered away at their individual stations.

Elspeth peered through the microscope at the tissue samples and studied the reports from the labs on the computer. The samples from the lab did not match the ones that she had just taken from the finger. In front of her, on another screen, she had open a number of research papers, all of them on anomalies concerning cell growth and repair. It was not just the difference between the samples that she was perplexed by: the cells themselves were of a type she did not recognise.

She called Matt over to have a closer look at something that had caught her eye:

"Come and have a look at this Matt," she urged, "Don't you think this looks like an accelerated rate of cell growth? Why would you see that...its almost like the finger is still growing..."

Matt stared down the scope. The samples continued to perplex him, as did the odd behaviour and speech patterns of the Shaz; why did they appear to be so deferential towards Ravi? It was not as if he was really someone that many people he knew wanted to emulate. it was all very odd.

"I think there's something going on here and we've nearly got it," said Matt. It's almost as if the Shaz are willing us to find out."

"Lets, get the finger out of its deep freeze," suggested Elspeth. The finger itself had been in the nitrogen drum for the past fifteen years, less the brief removal to take further samples for lab work. It was time for it to start its thaw.

Ellie had been online to one of her hacking contacts, the same person who had narrowed down the identity of coolio345londonboy. Fortunately for her, the hacker seemed to be always available (possibly permanently sitting in his bedroom, surrounded by empty soda cups, or, alternatively, some research scientist working from MIT or the like—who knew?). She needed another favour: fast. Was there any way that he could track down who coolio345londonboy had written to? She needed a name, not a user name; perhaps someone had used their own name as part of their 'tag'—johndoe or johndoe123, that kind of thing. Her contact said that he would get onto it straight away. The only real game in town was the takeover of the world by these weird creatures, and it was now known around the circuit that Ellie (or rather her online alter-ego) was connected in some way, so people wanted to help. Ellie took a deep breath and waited, this really was a last ditch attempt to pull something out of the bag.

Bruce was sitting in his study. He thought back through his years of research; he thought about the people who were trapped in the ship with the Shaz; he thought of the likelihood that the human race was not going to get out of this alive. Most of all he thought of his wife and grand-daughter, Ellie. He was running out of hope.

Brandon and Carl were talking in a room, away from the others.

"How are we going to get that little ship away from here?" asked Carl, "Get it to the same place as the other one?"

"Hold on, I'm thinking," replied Brandon, "We'll have to get that Ravi kid to send them over there. This seems to be linked to him."

"But they're not just gonna fly off just because he says so. He'll need a reason to get them there, and we'll need to go with him to check that it's gone to plan, otherwise the mission will have to be aborted till it can be set up," for Carl this was an awful lot of talking.

"Yeah, you're right, only the mission won't be so much aborted as changed." replied Brandon. "All we need to do is get the kid to go to that location near here where we saw the little things and get them to show up. SETU launch another mission there. We've been issued with full nuclear fallout gear."

"Jesus Christ, Brandon...That wasn't in the briefing." Carl sat down.

"I guess some things don't need to be broadcast until they happen, *if* they happen. OK?"

"OK."

"Now lets think how we're gonna get the kid out there."

RULES OF THE GAME

Ellie had received a reply from her contact. It had been hard, he said, but people had pulled out the stops when he'd revealed it was for her. He'd managed to dig deep into the archives held by servers for London local authorities and he'd found a couple of possible names: andy.thompson and rafiqhussein—could either of these be useful? He'd gone further: he'd managed to locate rafiq to an area called Sparkbrook in Birmingham and Andy could possibly be living in Eltham, south-east London. Her contact had included the last known contact details for both men. The possibility was that one of these young men could hold the key to the 'game' - if they could remember Ravi. Ravi and Ellie moved fast.

Ravi, recalled Andy and Rafiq as soon as he heard their names, so almost instantly he'd made some progress, though this fizzled away after this initial small success. He had been in the same tutor group with them in his GCSE year. That meant that the 'game' could have been about any subject, or none; it could have been a task set by the school for everyone in his year, perhaps a careers task, or the like. Try as he might, Ravi could still not get past the names.

Ravi called the number given for Rafiq—or Raf as he used to be called. The answer was not what he wanted to hear. Raf had gone to Pakistan to be with the family because one of his uncles had 'disappeared' and they were worried that the 'things' had taken him. Was there a number in Pakistan he could call him on, he asked? When he called the number he was given there was no answer. Ravi fired off a quick email and moved on, there was no time to waste chasing after ghosts and he just hoped that Andy proved more accessible.

Andy was, at least, in London Ravi discovered. Andy's

answering machine clicked onto the voice telling Ravi that Andy was 'not available' at present but suggested leaving a message and that Andy would 'get back to you as soon as possible' Ravi left one message, then two, he emailed the same email address from all those years ago and then, with Ellie's help, any personal or work address with 'Andy Thompson' in it for London. There was no answer. Out of desperation he called Angel.

"Listen," he had said to her, urgently, "Is there anyway you can get a ride over to this address in Eltham. I don't know if the guy's there, but I need to speak to him. This could be our last hope."

Angel had promised to get a friend to take her over there in a car (the tubes had been out for weeks) and park out in front of the address. All Ravi could do now was sit and wait.

It was late in the evening that Angel called Ravi on his mobile. She's been parked out in front of the ground floor maisonette for several hours. Doob had come with her, along with the friend that had driven; in the current climate it helped to have as many people with you as possible. They'd just seen someone about the right age walk into the flat, it could be the guy that he was looking for. What did Ravi want them to do now? Ravi thought for a while and then asked Angel to sit tight—he was going to try to call Andy again but if it didn't work he might need backup.

Andy answered the phone. He was wary at first, after all, things were so weird that everyone was on edge; what was there to say that the aliens weren't using the phone as a way to get to people? Ravi had to remind him of some of their exploits when they were at school together to win his confidence; even then Andy was not that trusting of Ravi.

"Yeah," Andy said, "OK, I remember you, Rav but...don't take this the wrong way, but why are you calling me? Don't you know that there's a pretty big crisis going down? You been locked in a sealed room for the past month or something?"

"Andy, I can't explain right now, but I've gotta ask you about when we were at school, y'know doing our GCSEs. This is gonna sound weird but do you remember doing any sort of project where I had the user name coolio345londonboy? Anything at all ring a bell...or do you remember anything about a game that I might have thought up?...it could even have been as part of our tutor group, you know in Mrs Scott's class." Ravi waited hopefully for the reply.

"No Ravi, I don't know what you're talking about. It was a long time ago and we all invented new user names every day. I don't know about any game—it could have been one of Mrs Scott's boring tutorial projects. I just dunno, all I can remember is that we had it drummed into us that we had to revise. Fat lot of good that did me. Anyway, look me up when you get back to London; if we ever get through this thing."

Andy hung up—he had BBC News 24 on in the background and he had just got word that people in outlying islands of Scotland were being evacuated for some reason, as was the entire population of Iceland and northern provinces of Canada. Something big was going down, he thought. This was getting serious.

Angel watched Andy put his phone down from outside the flat. She called Ravi straight back. "Do you need us for anything Ravi, can we help?"

Ravi told her to go home; as Andy had spoken his brain had slotted together most of the puzzle. He had remembered the game.

It was when Andy had mentioned revision that the penny had dropped. The 'game' had been an idea from some specialist performance improvement guru to try to improve exam results. It was one of a long lists of suggestions for how to revise: have a target, write notes, have regular breaks, avoid distractions, that sort of thing. Mrs Scott had asked them to think of a novel way to get people revising. Ravi had thought of this game—it was a bit of a joke really and he'd never put it into practice, but he'd got away with it as a legitimate effort for the task.

The idea was that you and some friends were supposed to devise a set of exam type questions on topics and then get the brainiest kids in school, for each subject, to tell you the answers You'd then have a brilliant set of answers to revise from. The theory was that if you thought up the questions you would get to recognise these on the exam paper, *and* you'd have forced all the bright kids to help you get model answers together...pretty neat huh?

It was a bit of a shabby, rough and ready thing as he could recall, you could ask whoever you liked to answer the questions, and there was no limit to the number of questions that could be asked. It was a rambling, confused, pig of a game and, though in the hands of a motivated group of students it might have had some useful purpose, in the hands of Ravi and his mates it served no purpose whatsoever.

Regardless, Ravi was certain that this was the game in question. This was the last thing that he had done in his tutor group before the year broke up for revision. It *had* to be this. The challenge was to determine how the game was being interpreted by the Shaz. How had they turned it from a humble mess of a set of confused rules into the rationale for kidnapping and killing a large (and seemingly never ending) succession of people.

Ravi and the team gathered together in the early hours. They didn't include Brandon and Carl; they wanted to keep this private. Ravi went through what he remembered about the game and threw it open to the others. What did people think was going on.

"Could the Shaz be grabbing people and asking some of them to think up questions and asking others for the answers?" suggested Ellie, "When people can't answer questions anymore maybe they are then seen as 'rejects' and sent back. Maybe they don't realise that people can't just keep answering endless questions?"

"What if they are expecting people to know the answers to questions that they have already got together? Those 'ancestors' you talked about, could have helped them" said Bruce, "You said that the Shaz said that they'd been **preparing** for the game, maybe they have been preparing by getting together a vast set of questions. What if, instead of the brightest kids in school, they abducted people who were good at one thing or another and might be able to answer questions on their 'thing'?"

"That sounds as if it might fit," agreed Ravi, "So, the Shaz capture people, attach them to these headphone set-ups, drain their brains of answers to all these questions...possibly to absorb the knowledge and then just 'reject' them. Because there is no 'winner' so to speak, there is no end point to the game, so the Shaz will just carry on going through more and more people."

"OK, this sounds like it just about might fit—and it's all we've got to go on" said Matt, "But can we use it to work out how we can stop the Shaz? I mean is there any way that you can call a halt to the game. Can we think of something that might convince them to stop, cos we all know this military thing isn't gonna work, don't we? Whoever the Shaz were calling on those monitors will be calling round pretty damn quick after the boom!"

They debated the possibilities for a couple of hours. Bruce suggested that they could just declare the game over. No good, said Ravi, he'd already asked them to stop and they'd taken no notice; there must be some sort of signal that they were waiting for—and he didn't know what it was. Ellie said that he could try to challenge the Shaz directly to the game, Ravi responded that, if they had been gathering a bank of knowledge for years, bearing in mind the fact that he had not exactly been topping up his knowledge reserves, it was not likely to be a contest that he could win, and anyway there wasn't really any 'winner' in the game.

What if you suggest a change of rules," suggested Ellie, after all, he was the 'games-master' if you like? That wouldn't work either, said Ravi—the Shaz had already said that things were unfair: they were clearly sticking with the instructions that they already had.

The only thing that they had seemed uncertain about was this 'friends' business, which seemed to crop up quite a lot. Ravi had no idea whether this was any use at all, but perhaps he could try and think of something that used this uncertainty to unsettle the Shaz? It was all quite hopeless. Eventually, in the early hours of the morning, Ravi decided to try and get to meet the Shaz and see if he could meet their 'leaders' at the base and 'wing it'—hoping that something would come to mind at the last minute. There was no other option left.

Brandon and Carl, listening through an earpiece in the other room breathed a sigh of relief; at the very least there was a chance that Ravi would lure the Shaz out to the road, hopefully he would take the little outpost party all the way back to their Greenland base. They might only need one strike after all.

The day dawned all too soon, with the sort of grey miserableness that epitomises a Scottish winter. The team had less than six hours to try and meet with the Shaz, to try to pull off what, at best could be described as a miracle result.

Across the world people were bracing themselves for something historic. The media had been pumping out announcements for people in 'affected areas' to make use of evacuation transport and not to try to stay in their homes, everyone else was being urged to stay in their homes to avoid being caught up in the 'operation'. This was serious stuff, made all the more frightening by the haste and somewhat hazy information. People looked up to the skies, holding their families close to them and praying. From the tiniest islands in the Pacific to the urban metropolises of North America, the world held its breath and waited.

In the small suburb of Edinburgh called Juniper Green, one household was not caught in the state of paralysis that had befallen the world. Bruce and Elspeth stayed at the house, both to monitor what was going on in the rest of the world and also because Elspeth felt that there was something she needed to check out about that finger—she had so nearly worked it out. Brandon and Carl were nowhere to be found.

Ravi, Ellie and Matt started on the road to the same, now familiar location to meet the Shaz. They knew that they would be there. They approached the street sign and slowed down, there was no sign of the Shaz.

"What if they don't show up?" said Ravi, losing his confidence, "They might know that something's not right."

"No, dude, they'll be here," said Matt, "I've been watching these things, watching the way that they behave...it's like they need to see you; they need the attention somehow."

Ellie agreed, "It's what we say to them when they do arrive that I'm worried about, Ravi. Just you focus on that, my friend."

Sure enough, the smallish white spacecraft glided silently in, settling as usual on the two walls either side of the road. The door to the craft opened and down slid the two Shaz that they had encountered a couple of days previously, they seemed to be permanent 'crew' on the transit vessel. The Shaz looked towards the group of young people with what could easily have been mistaken for friendship, indeed they seemed to have a particularly soft spot for Matt, who they attempted a sort of stubby wave towards. Matt half waved back.

"It is good to see you again, Ravi, Matt and Ellie, we are pleased that you are becoming our friends."

"Hey, that's OK, dudes; it's good to see you lot again too," said Matt and then realised that maybe he should have let Ravi take the lead, "Sorry, bro...over to you," he said to Ravi apologetically.

Ravi was just eager to get things moving. He had the feeling that they were running out of time. Whatever it was that SETU was planning would be well in progress now. If they were going to have any chance of resolving things any other way it had to be now. They had no time to lose.

The Shaz gestured for the three to come forwards and they boarded the craft.

"We'd like to go back to your base," suggested Ravi.

"Of course," agreed the Shaz, "We will be there very shortly."

In Utah things were reaching the final stages of preparation. The nuclear warheads had been checked and were locked onto their target in the Arctic Circle from their bases on the eastern side of Alaska, another smaller system was trained towards an area close to a small town in Falkirk, Scotland. In the operations room, an army of men in white shirt sleeves were watching screens, checking measurements and re-reading mails. In truth, they were all just waiting for the one command that would signal the change from 'ready' to 'go'. Everybody in the room understood the gravity of the task.

Gerry went from workstation to workstation, saying a little to an operator here and there. He knew how to be the all-American hero, all right. He was careful to slap one or two guys on the back and salute the generals and other military men. They might have the rank, he thought, but this was *his* moment of glory.

Agent Curtis was on the line, Gerry's secretary called out across the banks of desks. Would he like to take the video call on the floor, or in his office. Gerry made his way across the operations room, still encouraging his people over his shoulder, back to his office; if it was bad news, he thought, he wanted to be the only one to hear it.

Gerry needn't have been concerned, Brandon had excelled himself. Ravi was *at that exact moment* flying off to Greenland in the transit craft. He had followed the three young people and watched as they had boarded the craft and he'd *heard* Ravi agreeing the destination. There was no need for a second strike—hopefully. Gerry opened the door to where the world's defence leaders had gathered and played Brandon's message. There was relief that another target was not going to be in play but no premature celebration. The group knew that the future of the planet was on a knife edge. Gerry went back to his office and briefed the President. The staff on the floor looked up at his glass office walls, where he had left the blinds purposely lifted up. He saluted the President on the phone.

Gerry walked out again into the operations room, every set of eyes in the room following him as he walked down and took his seat at a control panel. The President had just given him the go ahead to set the process in motion and had input the agreed codes, in a co-ordinated exercise with other key world leaders, to start deployment and countdown. Gerry pressed a key on his control desk and the image on the massive monitor changed, from one showing time zones across the world and the route that their mission would take around the Arctic Circle, to one of simple counter. It was at fifty six minutes and counting.

ICY NORTH

Ravi and the others scurried across the ice bridge to the main ship where they were met by the welcoming party of Shaz dressed in red robes, those that Ravi had termed the elite of Shaz culture. Matt had insisted that his 'friends' from the other, smaller ship came with them this time. The mixed party—Shaz and human, looked down onto the cavernous middle section of the ship: the 'cube farm' where the prisoners were being kept.

"I want to talk about the game," Ravi said addressing the first 'red' Shaz, "The game that we've been playing together."

"You've not really been playing that much, Ravi; it was supposed to be a game for all of us." The Shaz sounded disappointed. "We are keeping to our side of the bargain but you are not really keeping to yours. "

Ravi thought for a minute. His strategy was multi-layered and it had taken a lot of brain-twisting to work it out—together with the help of the rest of the team. It was time to attempt the first layer. He nodded towards Matt.

"You know, I wanted to check something with you," Ravi said facing all three of the Shaz, "Do you have my original instructions?"

"Of course," said the Shaz, gleefully, "We always check anything that we do against the rules. That is why we are so disappointed that you seem to have ignored them."

Ravi looked serious, "That is because I have *forgotten* the rules. You see after I sent you the instructions I must have mislaid them; that is why I've been struggling with the rules and why you have had such poor opposition. If you remind me, I will be a much better player."

The Shaz looked convinced by this and, keen to improve the gameplay, waved a short arm at another member of the group to bring a copy of the rules as directed by coolio345londonboy in his direct communication with them. The Shaz scurried back and gave Ravi a sheet of paper that he looked at intently. He had remembered correctly.

"Ah-ha," he said knowingly, "I see that there has been some confusion about the instructions, yes, quite a bit of confusion!"

The Shaz looked at each other, rather worried, "Confusion?" they repeated.

"Yes...you see here where it says you can get your friends to help you set the questions." he paused, "Have you been doing that?"

The Shaz nodded and gestured towards the 'ancestors'. Bruce had been right, the small, but obviously special group had a hand in things too.

"Well, " he continued that's just one of those phrases that we use, isn't it Matt? When we say 'friends' in this context, we actually only meant just you three *higher* leaders," He gestured towards the Shaz in the red robes, "It's the same when it says 'as many questions as you like'...that actually means two questions per topic...'because 'as you like' refers to the rules of another game I thought up before this: a game I called 'You Like', which restricted questions to two per topic. After that I just used the phrase as sort of slang. Isn't that right Matt?"

Matt took on the role of key street-slang adviser to the Shaz, a role that built on his earlier and more honest, dialogue with the Shaz. He did a good job in trying to sound plausible about 'as many questions as you like' actually meaning 'two', all the time questioning how anyone would ever believe such an obvious load of rubbish. But the Shaz seemed genuinely unsure of themselves;

they called the oriental businesswoman 'ancestor' over and spoke to her very seriously. She appeared also to be concerned by what Ravi had said.

"Oh, and when I said that people who don't come up with enough answers are branded as 'rejects', that is another way that kids talk, on earth. I didn't mean *literally* branded as rejects!"

The Shaz looked worried. Had they been mistaken? Had they misinterpreted the rules that they had spent years studying? Had they really messed up the game that they had done so much preparation for?

"We ask for tolerance if we have got things wrong, but we will need to examine our records and see where we have not been accurate in our interpretations. We will then commence playing by the correct rules," suggested another one of the female 'red' Shaz.

"No can do, I'm afraid, we need to halt the game right now and free all of the human players," said Ravi, maintaining the momentum. He had his phone at the ready, in order to call Bruce to tell him the minute the people had been released, so that Bruce could tell Brandon to stop the SETU planned operation.

The Shaz looked mournful for a while but then one of them piped up. "In that case, we'll just have to get more players. We will send out for more as soon as we can."

This was not going to plan.

"No, no I don't think that I can allow that," said Ravi frantically, "What I mean is, the game has to be stopped now because you didn't play by the rules. You can't just make up for it at a later time, I'm afraid. You must let everyone go and go home."

The Shaz had huddled into a group and were talking amongst themselves in their own clicking spluttering language and seemed in no mood to give up. They didn't want to give up on their fun and were trying to work out a way around this setback.

Ravi could see the danger. He decided to play his trump card.

"There is no need to deliberate," he said to the gathered Shaz, "As you know there is already a mechanism for any disagreement about the rules. There is a final adjudicator."

The Shaz fell silent, then one of them said quietly, fearfully, "Mrs Scott."

"Yes Mrs Scott, " said Ravi, "It has taken me a long time to track down Mrs Scott but I've managed to locate her and I'm going to get her online now. Ravi had noticed that the Shaz had excellent internet coverage, even in the middle of nowhere and this seemed a safer bet that using a mobile. It had, however, meant a little bit of work on the part of the McLeish family.

Ravi opened up the notebook he had brought with him and connected to his destination. An image flashed up on the screen. It did look a *little* like Elspeth wearing a brown wig but they'd done quite a good job with the make-up. Ravi hoped that the Shaz had not taken that close an interest in Elspeth's appearance when they had seen her.

"Mrs Scott," acknowledged Ravi, "thanks for agreeing to adjudicate in the game." 'Mrs Scott' said it was no trouble at all—that was her role after all. Elspeth had been rehearsing the part since Ravi had recalled that he'd cited his form teacher as a sort of 'moderator' in the game. She fell naturally into the guise of a rather irritated Mrs Scott.

Ravi spelt out the problem to her: the rules had been broken, which was clearly unacceptable, furthermore the game, he said, was really meant to apply to the time period stipulated—from March to May of his exam year as laid out in the timetable attached to the original plan of the game. Therefore, the game was now being played in a completely unauthorised way and had to be halted.

"Yes, I see," said 'Mrs Scott, looking quite concerned about it all, "Well that sounds all very interesting...very *interesting*," she emphasised, "Well, what have you got to say for your side?" she asked the Shaz, peering at them over the half-rimmed glasses she had worn for the occasion. The Shaz, unprepared, could only say that it was a misunderstanding. However, they showed no sign whatsoever that they were going to free the captives. Their plan was, as they had told Ravi, to carry on playing the game with the 'new' rules.

This was so frustrating, thought Elspeth. It was such a rubbish game anyway, why on earth would anyone want to persevere with it? They were just acting like complete children. And then it hit her: their weird behaviour, the clueless and guilty look that they seemed to have much of the time, the stubbornness, the whispering to each other; it was all very *childish*. Mrs Scott mumbled something about being back in a few minutes as she needed to check on something and disappeared from the screen.

What on earth is going on? thought Ravi to himself: this wasn't in the script.

Elspeth had torn into her lab to look at something, she needed to check a few measurements that she had set up with Matt; she didn't have long but, as it happened, she didn't need long. She was right about the finger.

Why did they let us have it though? She asked herself, it doesn't make sense—not unless they are playing their *own* game with us.

She returned to the video-link and looked sternly at the Shaz.

"Well, I'm back," she said knowingly," and it's time to call it a draw. It is time for you children to end your little game and go home."

Elspeth had worked out that the Shaz were not fully grown— they were children. She and Matt had not understood the odd characteristics of the finger tissue samples, but, if one factored in maturity levels and growth, then the strange readings made sense. The Shaz that they had met were still growing—they were children. Everything seemed to make so much more sense once you understood this. That they had given Ravi and the others a clue about their deception: the gift of the finger, pointed to their wish to make things more interesting... to create a challenge for Ravi to work out for himself.

She was right. The Shaz had been found out.

"If you do not let all of the people go that you are keeping with you, I will personally report in to the rest of your kind—the grown-ups and tell them about this," Elspeth continued, growing more and more into her Mrs Scott role. "We have solved the challenge *and* you have lost our game by default. Now what's it to be: you shut up shop, let everyone go and go home...or I give the others a call." She looked towards an area of the deck where they could now work out what was on the video-links: *adult* versions of the Shaz.

"I bet they don't know what you've been up to," she said gesturing towards the screens, "You wouldn't want me to tell them now, would you?"

Ravi seized the moment.

"I declare this contest over by default," he said clearly and loudly. We have won both sides of the challenge and I, according to the rules and judgment of the adjudicator, require you to forfeit the people you are holding and leave immediately."

Within an astonishingly short amount of time the Shaz had transferred all of their prisoners onto the bleak ice-scape outside the space-craft. It was freezing cold and flurries of snow whirled around people as they huddled together to keep warm. They were, however, free. The giant Shaz base zoomed silently away, disappearing rapidly into the white sky. In what seemed like an instant, it was over.

Brandon was on the phone to Utah...”You can abort the mission, Sir. The aliens appear to have conceded defeat and gone home.”

The countdown at SETU was stopped with five minutes remaining.

GOING HOME

Ravi really liked Edinburgh. He liked the stylish sophistication and the slightly arrogant creativity about the place. He liked the fact that you could walk just about anywhere in town in what seemed like half an hour and the juxtoposition of the coast with the ancient city and the hills. It was a mystical, magical place and Ravi had discovered that he could be a different person there...but he was itching to get back to London. He and Matt had been in Edinburgh for some months now and spring was starting to make its presence felt, it was a time for change.

Things had taken a while to return to normal after the crisis. Initially, people did not believe that it was over and continued to monitor the airwaves for days, just to make sure. It was only when the released prisoners started appearing on news channels and talk shows that everyone really believed that it was safe to go back to the streets. Some people were still unconvinced and sales of paraphernalia aiming to guard against future invasion: protective shields, makeshift safe rooms and weapons found a massive new market.

There were still elements of the whole story that they didn't understand and probably never would.

None of the people who had been held on the 'cube farm' seemed to remember much after a few days (thankfully, said the psychologists), but appeared to have been under intense psychological pressure in some process that tapped into their through processes. Long-term tests would be needed but, so far, no brain-damage was detected. In a deeper sense, they would never be the same again.

What was the significance of the headphones left for Ravi and the bracelet given to him by the Indian girl ancestor? The headphones—well they seemed to be some sort of witty clue and the 'ancestors', still baffled them. Who were the ancestors and what happened to them? They didn't strike Ravi as being mercenaries and were too 'human' to be part of the Shaz. There was no sign of them amongst the people released from the ship. Angel told them that Carlo had spotted the guy that left the package for Ravi again, hanging around Beluga, but then again there were plenty of guys fitting his description in that part of London.

There was the tragedy of the people who had been 'rejected' and had lost their lives, amongst them citizens of all the countries on earth. A memorial was planned for the victims to honour their names forever as innocent victims. Ravi, Ellie and the others had been asked to attend as guests of honour.

Predictably, interest in the three of them was high. The scientific community was eager to explore as much as possible about what they had seen on board the Shaz's space-craft and even more keen to know about their conversations with the Shaz. People from the shadowy world of defence put them under intense surveillance and pressure for some time. Ravi and the others mastered the art of diplomacy and only revealed the bare minimum. They had no interest in becoming research subjects of either science or the government.

Ellie, Ravi and Matt strolled alongside the Water of Leith and on through Dean Village to the Old Town. There, they stopped at one of Ellie's favourite pubs in the shadow of Edinburgh University. Huddled together in an alcove, they felt like three gnarled old adventurers just returned from some epic voyage.

"It's all a bit much, this," said Matt after a few slugs of beer, "The Shaz have gone now and I don't think they'll be coming back, so what's the point of us being here? I mean all this ducking and diving to shake off one agency or another is doing my head in! I just wanna, like, go and hide out back home now. Just chill and stuff. "

"London calling?" suggested Ravi.

"Spot on bro...I need to be back in the big smoke."

They both looked at Ellie for confirmation of their travel plans.

"Hey, every big adventure's got to end sometime..." she agreed, "or maybe it's time for another one."

"Give me a break!" laughed Ravi.

Back in London, Ravi was home. There were the familiar sounds, smells and sights and also some changes. London itself seemed different, as if it had become smaller somehow, it had become somewhere that you could now see over the edge of.

Ravi didn't go back to his mobile phone job, he and Matt decided that they were going to start something of their own. They'd been given some money by a couple of the networks in the US for saying a few things about the 'alien invasion' (what they said was, to be honest, made up, but the channels had seemed more than happy with their performance) and were considering starting a niche company offering 'alternative' tours of London—to include destinations like Big Frankie's and Beluga. Despite having little business experience, they decided that their combination of skills: being laid back, knowing East London and getting the word out on the street about stuff was ideal as a starting point.

Ellie, Ravi and Matt had each been visited individually by a serious looking woman from a 'government agency' who suggested that there was a place for them with a special team' if they wanted to continue their work with extra-terrestrials and interplanetary phenomena. It was clear to the agency that they had the potential to make a real difference to a number of missions. Matt and Ravi declined and Ellie—well she declined also, but that didn't mean that she wasn't involved in the field...

Ellie decided to move into a small flat of her own, not too far away. She'd come back to visit the guys often, to 'keep an eye on them', as she said. To be honest her favourite thing was to tube it over to Holly Road and settle down for some pizza and a heavy dose of Playstation, Doob's tunes thudding through the walls. Doob had moved back into the flat and had taken up the producer opportunity with Jammo. The gig was going well and he was also going to get in with the tour thing that Ravi and Matt were setting up—that or taking his music to the US. For a while they all just wanted to enjoy being young.

That Autumn and Winter marked a rite of passage for the team. Behind the scenes they were preparing. The wheels of another adventure were turning. Life would never be the same again.

ABOUT THE AUTHOR

Franklin Zebb is a writer living in the United Kingdom. Franklin's life has included music management, performance sport and living with indigenous communities in far-flung corners of the globe.

Franklin's writing observes the real and imaginary worlds. Sometimes witty, sometimes dark; Franklin is a master of the almost believable.

www.ingramcontent.com/pod-product-compliance
Lightning Source LLC
Chambersburg PA
CBHW061339160726
47995CB00001B/94